ON MEDIA

ON POLITICS
L. Sandy Maisel, Series Editor

On Politics is a new series of short reflections by major scholars on key subfields within political science. Books in the series are personal and practical as well as informed by years of scholarship and deliberation. General readers who want a considered overview of a field as well as students who need a launching platform for new research will find these books a good place to start. Designed for personal libraries as well as student backpacks, these smart books are small format, easy reading, aesthetically pleasing, and affordable.

Titles in the Series

Forthcoming in the Series

DORIS GRABER

ON MEDIA

MAKING SENSE OF POLITICS

Paradigm Publishers
Boulder • London

Copyright © 2012 by Paradigm Publishers

Published in the United States by Paradigm Publishers, 2845 Wilderness Place, Boulder, Colorado 80301 USA.

Paradigm Publishers is the trade name of Birkenkamp & Company, LLC, Dean Birkenkamp, President and Publisher.

Library of Congress Cataloging-in-Publication Data

Graber, Doris A. (Doris Appel), 1923–
  On media : making sense of politics / Doris A. Graber.
    p. cm. — (On politics)
  Includes bibliographical references and index.
  ISBN 978-1-59451-474-6 (hardcover : alk. paper) —
ISBN 978-1-59451-475-3 (pbk. : alk. paper)
  1. Mass media—Political aspects—United States. 2. Television broadcasting of news—United States. 3. Political socialization—United States. 4. Political participation—United States. 5. Communication in politics. 6. Television programs—Political aspects—United States. 7. Mass media—Political aspects—United States—Case studies. I. Title.
  PN4888.P6G63 2011
  302.230973—dc23

                                                    2011022077

Printed and bound in the United States of America on acid-free paper that meets the standards of the American National Standard for Permanence of Paper for Printed Library Materials.

Designed and Typeset by Straight Creek Bookmakers.

16 15 14 13 12   5 4 3 2 1

This book is a tribute to my beloved, story-telling mom and a welcome to young Ianos to the wonders of story lands.

CONTENTS

PREFACE

There is a story behind every book, and *On Media: Making Sense of Politics* is no exception. This tale, though, starts earlier than most. When I was growing up, bedtime was story time. My mother, who was a talented landscape painter, was also a wonderful storyteller. She invented new stories every night, and somehow managed to connect them to the events of that day. There was always a lesson in them—not blatantly, but it would pop out whenever I thought about the story and wondered what was coming next.

I learned a lot from those stories without realizing that I was learning. I also had pictures in my head about the critters in the stories, because my mother described them so vividly. The talking frogs were real, and so were the chirping baby birds, the magic Persian flying carpets, and the poor, emaciated children in India who would love to have the food that I had left on my plate the night before.

In the larger scheme of things, what my mother taught me was the importance of learning from good stories that create new worlds that listeners and watchers can actually experience, even if only for brief spans of time. If children can learn from well-told and image-rich stories, why can't grown-ups?

Fast-forward to me as an adult academic who studies political communication with a keen interest in the ways that humans process information, and learn from what they see and hear. My research and writings have focused on information dispensed by the most popular news medium: nightly news broadcasts.

As a citizen, I am worried about the implications of studies that argue that average Americans are ignorant about the political issues facing their communities. Surveys clearly show that fewer citizens watch the nightly news. The shrinkage of news audiences is precipitous, with no evidence that the defectors are flocking *en masse* to alternative newscasts.

From my past research, I know that many people from all walks of life and all levels of formal education do care about politics, and that they understand quite a bit about it. Like many of my friends, I have marveled at the shrewd political analyses that taxi drivers can offer *en route* to town or to and from airports. Where do they, and the many other people I converse with in the course of a year, get their political information and their keen insights? Could it come from the fictional serial dramas that they routinely watch on television? In light of my childhood experiences, it seemed worth investigating.

That is how this book began. It started with a study of the political themes in television dramas like the *Sopranos,* which features an organized crime syndicate, medical shows like *Grey's Anatomy,* and cartoon shows about small-town life like *The Simpsons.* I owe a debt of gratitude to the students who watched hundreds of episodes of various dramas. They systematically recorded detailed observations about the meanings conveyed by the pictures, words, and sounds.

The content analyses of drama episodes revealed that most shows contained significant political messages, either directly in their story lines or indirectly in the environments that they portrayed. But, as in my mother's stories, the lessons were rarely blatant, except for the *The West Wing,* which was staged in a White House setting and covered a fictional president.

Did the political lessons from the dramas actually surface in viewers' minds, or were they drowned out by the story line? To find out, we decided to interview habitual viewers of the shows. That meant adding interviewers to the research team. They contacted respondents and administered the interviews, as laid out by the research design. Numerous "scouts" helped us locate suitable interview targets, namely faithful viewers of one of the content-analyzed serial dramas.

The list of scouts is too long to mention. But the interviewer list is short and important enough to record. Thanks are due to Brooke Cadwell and Gretchen Graber, and to graduate students Kevin Navratil and especially Gregory Holyk. Besides conducting interviews in various group settings, Gregory, now Dr. Holyk, also performed important quantitative and qualitative data analyses for the study.

The next stage of the research project was a matter of sheer good luck. When I lectured at the University of Leiden in the Netherlands in 2006, I had the good fortune to meet a colleague and now good friend Dr. Tereza Capelos, who is a specialist in political psychology. Dr. Capelos offered to match the interviews done in the United States with interviews and similar analyses in the Netherlands, where these shows are syndicated. She also enlisted the help of Professor Nicolas Demertzis of the University of Athens to do a similar companion study in Greece. Kostas Vadratsikas, Sander Ensink, Dunya van Troost, Mischa Tan, and Lisette Heijer—all of the University of Leiden—assisted with the interviews, which were conducted in the local languages. Special thanks go to Kostas, who led the Greek and Dutch teams, and contributed significantly to the qualitative analyses of the Greek interviews.

It is not uncommon for strokes of good fortune to be over-whelmed by personal tragedies. In my case, the tragedy was the terminal illness and ultimately death in 2007 of my husband, who was my best friend, my strongest supporter, and my lifetime companion. When that happened, the *On Media: Making Sense of Politics* manuscript, like Snow White of fairy-tale fame, went into a deep slumber. I finally restored it back to life because it was a cherished study that I was eager to share with students and peers. The unfailing support that Jennifer Knerr, Vice President and Executive Editor of Paradigm Press, gave to the book also played a crucial part in its revival. Her patience in waiting for manuscript copy was legendary, as was her skill in pointing out weaknesses and suggesting alternatives. During the final writing stages Amy Beth

Schoenecker, my graduate assistant, gave me valuable research help. Graduate students Katherine Griffiths, Melanie Mierzejewski, and James M. Smith also deserve mention for their major contributions to the chapters about public opinions and about news media content. I thank all of the contributors to the book, as well as the American, Dutch, and Greek interview subjects, who must remain anonymous. Like a tree, a book cannot grow without the roots that sustain it.

Finally, I thank the production team, especially Candace English and Marilyn Smith, for eagle eyes that found the gremlins in the manuscript and chased most of them away. I take responsibility for the ones that are left or crept stealthily into the book during production.

INTRODUCTION

On Media: Making Sense of Politics is a multifaceted book. It begins and ends with clear evidence that average people can understand politics, even when their memories are short on specifics.

The book refutes widespread charges that average Americans do not understand politics and that they care little about the major political issues that face them as citizens. It features reports about a series of research projects that support the main arguments in different ways and from different perspectives.

Each chapter tells a complete story. You, the reader, can choose where you wish to pick up the trail. Here, I provide a map for the journey. It offers brief glimpses of some of the sites that the chapters visit, and a tiny sample of the kinds of reasoning and assumptions that you are likely to encounter along the way.

Can Average Americans Make Sense of Politics?

The essence of research findings depends on the appropriateness and quality of the research tools. This is why Chapter One starts with a crucial issue concerning scientific measurements. Have researchers used the correct tools when measuring whether people are smart or dumb about politics? The answer to that question is important because democratic governments should be guided by citizens who are knowledgeable about what they want and need from their political institutions. Chapter One explains how and why many prominent social scientists are using the wrong kinds of yard-sticks for assessing citizens' political savvy and civic competence.

The chapter delves into the heated controversies over what modern citizens, individually and collectively, can and should know to perform their civic duties properly. Here, and throughout the remainder of the book, I argue that discussions about these cru-cial issues must proceed on a realistic level, rather than from the idealistic perspectives that are so dear to the hearts of democratic theorists.

Analysts must take account of the realities of political life in highly complex modern societies, and have full awareness of the functions that citizens actually perform. Arguments must also be grounded in the physiological and psychological limitations and proclivities of average adults in the society where civic intelligence is measured.

Chapter One ends with a demonstration of civic competence at the collective level, where individual views are blended into public opinions. It traces major changes in the balance of public opinion verdicts about four important public policy questions. These changes demonstrate that citizens keep abreast of key politi-cal developments and alter their views when conditions warrant it.

The Adequacy of the News Supply

The second chapter evaluates the adequacy and quality of the news that is readily available to the American public. The assessments consider the context surrounding each news story. For example, a very brief article about revolution in Egypt may be short on crucial facts, but it might be quite adequate at the time of publication, if it merely updates extensive news stories published earlier.

The data in this chapter comes from a comprehensive content analysis of one week's news coverage of citizenship-relevant sto-ries published by major sources of current information. Sources included newspapers, over-the-air local and national newscasts, cable newscasts, assorted news talk shows, nationally syndicated radio programs, and well-known liberal and conservative blogs.

The research identifies the type of political content readily available to average Americans. It appraises to what extent the content provides a basis for developing common political priorities that nourish a sense of political community.

The chapter stresses the importance of judging the news supply from both individual and collective perspectives. Individuals need not, and cannot, know about everything, and individual news venues need not, and cannot, cover everything. But collectively, the public needs to know about essential topics, and news media collectively must provide ample coverage of them.

The most interesting, important, and surprising finding reported in Chapter Two concerns the breadth of coverage. The totality of news was far more adequate than anticipated. That optimistic finding is muted somewhat by evidence that the quality of news is all too often overly thin.

Chapter Two, like the other chapters, takes a few side trips to shed additional light on the public's political savvy in relation to the streams of available information. When people are called ignorant because they give wrong answers to polling questions, the pollsters, rather than the public, may be at fault. Investigations of the match between polling questions and the relevant information supply reveal that questions often do not match the information that news media offer to the public. Moreover, the questions may be inherently unfair, because correct answers might require complex, often controversial calculations that are beyond the capabilities of nonexperts.

Television Dramas as News Sources

Chapter Three is the gateway to the most seminal part of the book: the analysis of prime-time television serial dramas as sources of political information for millions of citizens from all walks of life.

The chapter opens with a discussion of the many features that make these dramas such excellent venues for transmitting information that viewers learn and remember. It describes how the research was designed and what was done to conduct that research. It supplies details about the traditional experiments, the nontraditional semistructured telephone interviews, and the content analysis of Internet message boards. It also explains the reasons for unconventional features of the research. Like other chapters, it points out the political implications of the research findings.

Insights about Television Dramas: What Americans Told Us

Chapter Four gives an overview of the data culled from the interviews. It puts them into the larger context of how, what, and why people learn from the political environment that surrounds them. It offers a large-scale map, so to speak, of the intellectual territory that will be put under the microscope in later chapters.

Chapter Four begins with analyses of the political information that was embedded in the nine shows on which the interviews were based. Four of these—*The West Wing, The Simpsons, ER,* and *The Sopranos*—are presented as examples of the different types of learning environments that each show provides. Clearly, some dramas offer rich, well-balanced information diets that give people important insights; others feature junk-food or starvation diets. Some of the political lessons embedded in the dramas are rich and easy to consume; others let trivial details of the story overpower the larger meanings. Like nonfiction newscasts, most dramas offer a mixed bag, ranging from highly sophisticated political insights to misleading impressions.

The chapter provides an overview of the kinds of knowledge that drama watchers are likely to absorb from watching show episodes. It exposes the difficulties that researchers face when they try to discover what is in people's minds, how deeply or superficially it is embedded, how strongly it stirs various emotions, and what the connections are among various streams of knowledge. Sadly, research about the civic IQ still can do little more than illuminate specific targets. Like a flashlight, it leaves the surroundings in the dark.

Prime-time television dramas are potent cultural forces in the United States and elsewhere. Chapter Four tells how news media report about the dramas, and how they often compare actual political happenings to their fictional counterparts. Homer Simpson and Jack Bauer are well-known public figures in the United States. Encyclopedias and websites carry special entries for them that are updated throughout the life of the shows, and even their reruns following the final episodes. Such prominence has political consequences.

Learning from Television Dramas: What Europeans Told Us

Chapter Five reports the systematic, detailed analyses of the actual interview transcripts. It matches them with results from companion studies carried out in the Netherlands and in Greece that used the same stimulus dramas, the same questions with a few supplements, and the same interviewing procedures.

The European studies were intended to test learning from prime-time television serial dramas in related yet different cultures to find out whether the American findings are culture-specific. The chapter shows how the European findings differ from their American counterparts, and how compatible they are with the belief that learning differs across political cultures.

Looking Back and Looking Forward

The concluding chapter puts the concept of learning under the microscope. Based on the evidence in earlier chapters, it describes and analyzes seven different types of learning. These range from learning major and minor facts to comprehending the interplay of political factors and drawing fresh conclusions. The chapter provides specific examples and reports the relative frequency of these factors. It discusses how they affect people's comprehension of their political world.

The chapter also highlights the factors that are important in arousing viewer attention to news messages, because paying attention is a prerequisite for learning. Most information broadcast on the Internet and elsewhere amounts to never-heard cries in the wilderness. This is why Chapter Five reports research that assesses how various types of information offerings can attract the attention of potential audiences. The chapter notes the significance of various contextual conditions that can encourage or discourage learning. It shows that human learning depends not only on the content and framing of the message, but hinges equally on the context that surrounds audience members when they receive particular information.

The sensitive, reality-based, multimethod research approaches used for collecting the data for *On Media: Making Sense of Politics* have revealed many facets of political learning that more traditional studies fail to consider. The chapter ends with a few recommendations for making political information in nonfiction news stories more user-friendly, so that citizens will find it easier to assess the political scene and develop and express their political preferences.

May your journey through this book about political learning be productive, enjoyable, and memorable. When you watch the next episode of your favorite television drama, remember that it is far more than just entertainment. More or less, it is also an important and lasting lesson about the vagaries of real-life current politics!

CHAPTER ONE
CAN AVERAGE AMERICANS MAKE SENSE OF POLITICS?

America's founders fully understood that an informed citizenry is essential for democratic governance. They believed that citizens would be willing and able to guide their government's public policies. They also understood the crucial role that a free and responsible press, insulated from undue government influence, could play in informing citizens about their political world.

Throughout the nation's history, the faith in the essential soundness of citizens' opinions has never waned. Concern about ensuring an ample flow of political information has also persisted, because citizens must be sufficiently well informed to perform their civic responsibilities adequately.

Much of my research has focused on these crucial issues. The book puts making sense of politics under the microscope, looking at evidence about the soundness of political opinions, the adequacy of the political information supply, and the many tools people use to gain insights about the world in which they live.

The opening pages of this first chapter deal with key issues that have surfaced in the hot debates about whether average Americans are hopelessly dumb or reasonably smart when it comes to politics. This chapter also calls attention to the important distinctions between citizens' civic competence at the individual level and civic competence at the collective "public-opinion" level. The chapter ends with a series of reports that demonstrate that Americans still follow news about politics, despite a new, distracting media environment.

Setting the Scene

When social scientists test citizens' knowledge, what kinds of questions do they ask, and should they ask them? And what kinds of questions do they shun, and should they shun them? Should they measure political intelligence in some abstract way, and if so, what should be their measures? Alternatively, should the scales be related to the actual tasks of citizenship in twenty-first century America?

Idealism Versus Realism

My research on citizens' capacity to make sense of politics has sparked much of my criticism of current political science studies that assess the quality of citizens' level of political knowledge, as well as their capabilities and inclinations to perform their civic duties. These studies allege that citizens are politically ignorant, unable to make sound political judgments, and generally apathetic when it comes to political matters. I have questioned the validity of such claims because most current measurement standards ignore the realities of personal and political life in highly complex modern societies. They also ignore the physiological and psychological factors that limit learning, and the fact that average American adults lack a passion for politics. Instead, the critics focus normatively on what citizens ought to know and do in the imaginary ideal, yet unreal, world of democratic theories.

In the ideal world, citizens should be interested in all major activities undertaken by their governments. They should keep up with detailed, fact-studded, current information, remember the past, and when surveyed, be able to accurately answer the kinds of questions that might earn them a good grade in survey courses of American government and politics. Alas, most citizens fall precipitously below these idealistic standards!

Idealism is great, but the stark realities of life move most ideals beyond reach. To keep pace with developments in the real world, ideals and standards for measuring citizens' civic performance must keep pace with changing real-life conditions. Democratic citizenship in a large, modern state in the twenty-first century is a far different challenge than the demands faced by citizens in earlier historical periods. Comparing governing the ancient city state of Athens, where democracy originated around 500 BC, with governing modern Greece or the current United States is as meaningful as comparing a Tinkertoy airplane with a modern four-engine airliner like the double-deck, wide-bodied Airbus A380. The scales of construction and operation are incomparable.

Throughout much of recorded history, government functions were limited to defending the borders of the terrain that the governing powers claimed as their own. In the twenty-first century, government-enforced rules and regulations cover nearly all aspects of citizens' lives—from external security to internal security, public and individual health, education, Social Security benefits, protection of the environment, and on and on. The number of public officials has grown accordingly, as has the segmentation of their work into specialized tasks. Roughly 8 percent of the 155 million working Americans hold government jobs in literally hundreds of different job categories.

The explosive growth of government organizations and functions has dramatically changed the roles that most citizens can play in democratically governed societies. When government officials are forced to become specialists, trained to perform very complex functions, citizens must narrow down their roles as well. At best, they can master the intricacies of only a few public-policy areas, while maintaining an overall, nonspecific, superficial understanding of others.

As political scientist Thomas Patterson put it eloquently in his study of the role of the press and its failure to supply the types of news that the public can understand, "Citizens are not Aristotles who fill their time studying politics. People have full lives to lead: children to raise, jobs to perform, skills to acquire, leisure activities to pursue. People have little time for attending to politics in their daily lives, and their appetite for political information is weak" (Patterson, 1993: p. 45).

The Age of the Monitorial Citizen

Michael Schudson, a Harvard-trained sociologist, wrestled extensively with the problems of effective citizenship under various historical circumstances. In his 1998 book-length study, *The Good Citizen: A History of American Civic Life,* he points out that it has become impossible in the current age for citizens to play the role of the fully "informed citizen" as envisioned by political theorists. Ready access to an array of news media does not mean that citizens can become adequately informed about the full panoply of current major political issues, and that they can form, and possibly express, well-reasoned opinions about all policy options. That realization paved the way for Schudson to develop the concept of the *monitorial citizen.*

Monitorial citizens do not need to know about every major issue facing the country because there are too many issues and their complexity is overwhelming. Instead, monitorial citizens "should be informed enough and alert enough to identify danger to their personal good and danger to the public good. When such danger appears on the horizon, they should have the resources ... to jump into the fray and make a lot of noise" (Schudson, 1998: p. 23). That makes the press, which is citizens' main source of information, "... a tool of civic life. It is a necessary tool. The media's main task is critique, monitoring, a watchdog over authority" (p. 23).

Schudson does not stress many of the factors of modern political life that must be considered in appraising how well monitorial citizens are performing. For instance, analysts must bear in mind that modern citizens' civic concerns are focused mostly on happenings close to home, rather than at the national or international level. Also, monitorial citizens are apt to concentrate on personally relevant economic and social issues, at the expense of the issues that are at the center of elected national officials' concerns at the time.

When citizens monitor and participate at the local level, which is an important political arena, they may not have time to engage extensively at the national level. But knowledge about subnational politics is rarely measured in the United States. Citizens are labeled as political dummies, even when their low scores on tests about national politics mask high levels of knowledge about local politics.

Schudson also does not highlight the fact that collective public opinions can still be sound, even when many individual opinions are flawed. A blended product, like public opinion, takes on its own identity that smoothes out the incongruity of many of its parts. That reality must be kept in mind when assessing what individual citizens ought to know. Even when only 54 percent of citizens knew the precise level of unemployment in 2010, the collective level of knowledge was high enough to deserve respect for citizens' judgment that the issue should become a higher priority on the government's action agenda (Pew Research Center, 2010a).

Assessment of the adequacy of citizens' individual civic capacity must also consider the roles that individual citizens play. Public officials, like the mayor of the City of Chicago or the members of the Chicago City Council, need to know a great deal more than ordinary Chicagoans who play comparatively minor political roles. Knowledge needs vary depending on individuals' concerns and their positions in society, and individuals focus their learning accordingly. Tests of civic competency should reflect these variations.

What Monitorial Citizens Need to Know and How They Learn It

It is a tough challenge to determine what monitorial citizens *need* to know and what they *can* know, considering the complexities of modern life. How can they perform their citizenship functions adequately when their resources of time and energy are limited? When we tackle this challenge from a realistic and pragmatic perspective, the question becomes, "What is doable for average citizens and sufficient to maintain well-functioning governments?"

The framers of the American Constitution opted for representative rather than direct democracy. That means that citizens do not act as legislators and administrators. Instead, they elect representatives as their agents for making political decisions and for the actual governing. Their electoral choices must be good. Therefore, during elections, citizens need information about the candidates' character, qualifications, and policy views, so that they can use their people-judging skills to make good choices. In between elections, citizens must have sufficient information about salient policy options and their agents' performance to know when there are serious lapses in the quality of performance, when misdeeds are suspected, or when policies run counter to their wishes.

To gather the necessary information, citizens must keep in touch, directly or indirectly, with news media about stories that will alert them to issues and people that require attention. Given the large amounts of available news, individual citizens must winnow it down, focusing on what interests them and what they think they need to know for the sake of their family, job, and community.

In the modern world, the political generalists of earlier generations who were familiar with most aspects of government have been replaced by citizens who focus on a limited number of concerns. Modern American governance requires a variety of specialized publics who monitor a small number of political issues at the local, state, regional, or national level. What matters is that, collectively, all levels of politics and all types of issues receive some scrutiny.

Even within the specialized areas, citizens' duties must fit into the limits of tight time and energy budgets, because these precious resources should be conserved. Expectations and calculations should be realistic. In countries like the United States, where citizens number into hundreds of millions, specialization is quite feasible. Some people may focus on education issues, the environment, or relations with China, while others attend more to health care, credit-card fees, or gun-control laws. Collectively, these citizens can keep track of the country's main public policy concerns.

Monitoring major political problems is made easier because most have long histories. Similar events have happened before. Public records include stories about past successes and failures that provide clues to what works and what is likely to flop. The specifics and the actors change, but the main challenges remain fairly constant.

For example, public health and sanitation issues have been long-standing, including questions about the appropriate scope of government activity and the levels of enforcement. That means that citizens have developed attitudes about problems like compulsory vaccinations, chemical additives to the water supply, and oversight of public campgrounds. Citizens can use these stored opinions when they must make new judgments. They have also learned to ease and shorten the political judgment process by using heuristics.

Using Heuristics to Make Choices

Heuristics are shortcuts for decision-making. They consist of indicators that citizens learn to identify and use as cues for judging the political scene.

For example, when faced with puzzling political issues, citizens may simply adopt the views of trusted opinion leaders whose political astuteness they respect. Some citizens may summarily reject all policies that require borrowing money or seem highly expensive. People may learn these cues during their formal schooling, through personal experiences, or through discussions with others. Political scientist Samuel Popkin calls the process "low informational rationality" (Popkin and Dimock, 1999). He describes it as people's ability to use minimal information, like general knowledge about the main differences between political parties, to make reasonable political choices about particular policies that are important to them.

Social scientists who believe that "rational" choices should guide citizens' political judgments often disparage the use of heuristics. But, in fact, using readily available cues to make political judgments in complex situations constitutes very rational behavior. It would be far too costly in time and other resources for most citizens to acquire enough detailed information to make their own fully considered judgments. When issues are very complex, it usually makes more sense for citizens to rely on experienced advisors' judgments than to develop their own conclusions about issue areas that are beyond their expertise.

News Stories as Sources of Information

News stories and the opinions that they reflect can be valuable sources for forming individual political views, especially when the news stories quote a diverse array of experts and the reasons that these experts give to support their claims. Citizens can choose to concentrate on the facts provided by news stories, weigh the various justifications, and then try to form their own opinions about the meaning of these facts. Alternatively, they can use the stories as leads to heuristic cues.

For example, news audiences can simply adopt the perspectives provided by one of the sources cited in the story, based on that source's ethnicity, age, gender, or occupation. Or they can take the advice provided by the reporters who have written the story.

As is the case in all complex decision-making, a sound process does not guarantee a sound outcome. Even when great care is taken in weighing essential factors, the conclusions drawn from reported facts may still be only partly right, or they may be entirely wrong and occasionally disastrous. Besides, soundness lies in the eye of the beholder. Policies hailed by an incumbent government as perfect and highly beneficial for the public may be condemned by the government's opponents as misguided, harmful efforts.

Making judgments based on information from news stories—or any other source, for that matter—is always error-prone. Most complex situations involve far more facts than news stories, including eye-witness accounts, can present. That forces reporters to select the facts that they deem most important. Among others, these choices may be based on the reporters' predispositions, their views about what the prospective audience wants to hear, and the ease with which certain elements in the story can be discovered and explained. Depending on the choice criteria, the facts that are made available will vary. The judgments that citizens make, based on this extract from the full pool of information, may be quite different than the judgments that they would make if they knew all the facts.

Collective public opinion benefits from the fact that the individual opinions that it merges tap into substantially different information bases, which, as the next chapter shows, span a very broad array of public concerns.

The Civic IQ Paradigm: Memorization Versus Understanding

When judging the capabilities of citizens to evaluate their political environment and perform citizenship functions, individually or collectively, scholars often talk about the *civic IQ.* The term refers to people's understanding of the political world in which they live and their ability to determine the significance of various situations (Graber, 2001).

Understanding involves much more than knowing specific political facts. It involves citizens' ability to incorporate their own experiences and intuitions about politics into how they think about their political environment, as well as how they assess their political needs and reconcile them with their civic and personal obligations. A low civic IQ signifies a lack of understanding of your political surroundings, inability to make sense of political information or describe political phenomena, and inability to adapt your life to your political environment.

The major regime changes that citizens in many countries encountered in the twentieth century were testing grounds for their civic IQ. Passage from democratic regimes to communist regimes and back again provides many examples. Most citizens passed the test. Some failed, and they often paid with their lives for their failure. At the core of civic IQ is intelligence. It includes capacities such as comprehension, learning, and problem-solving. Civic IQ encompasses parallel concepts such as the following:

- *Social intelligence,* which is the ability to understand and manage others (Thorndike, 1920; Goleman, 2006)
- *Interpersonal intelligence,* which is the ability to comprehend the intentions, motives, and desires of others
- *Intrapersonal intelligence,* which involves the ability to understand yourself and to assess your personal emotions, fears, or motives (Gardner, 1975)
- *Emotional intelligence,* which is the ability to gauge how emotions determine your own and others' thinking and actions (Salovey and Mayer, 1990; Goleman, 1995)

Measuring the Civic IQ

Political scientists who favor rational choice tenets believe that citizens cannot make sound political choices unless they remember precise facts about political situations. Therefore, they measure the civic IQ with closed-ended factual knowledge questions. Studies by Michael Delli Carpini and Scott Keeter provide excellent examples, starting with their landmark 1996 book, *What Americans Know about Politics and Why It Matters.*

The highly regarded National Election Studies (NES) surveys rate citizens' political knowledge on a four-point name recognition scale. Respondents are questioned about four politically prominent individuals. The survey provides four names and asks, "What job or political office does he now hold?" The names belong to the Speaker of the House of Representatives in Congress, the U.S. Vice President, the Chief Justice of the U.S. Supreme Court, and the British Prime Minister. The responses are disappointing. They show that citizens are poorly informed about politics when knowledge is measured by the accuracy of answers to factual knowledge questions that require recalling specific names or numbers associated with political situations. Analysts then conclude that average Americans do not understand how the political process works, fail to form reasoned opinions about important and widely publicized political issues, and hold a lot of misconceptions. If this were true, government by public opinion would be a tragic farce.

Fortunately, the work of many other scholars, including my research, demonstrates that the harsh judgments about citizens' civic IQ are wrong. The factual questions that lead to these judgments are unsuitable for assessing the understanding that lies at the heart of the civic IQ. A broad understanding of political processes and likely political outcomes does not hinge on memorizing specific numbers and names. It hinges on the ability to apply past experiences to current situations, and then assess their meaning and significance.

The expectation that individuals should be able to recall the specific data that gave rise to their political opinions runs counter to human physiological and psychological functioning. When people encounter news, efficient human thinking requires compacting or forgetting most details, and merely storing the meanings extracted from the news, because the average human brain's capacity to keep information on tap for rapid recall is limited (Graber, 2001). After humans have constructed meanings from news, the message details fade from readily accessible memory. People are conserving their precious memory resources. Recall scores about specific events are highest at the time when the event is occurring or when it has been recently highlighted again.

Specific message meanings that individuals store vary because they are merged with the information that each person already holds in memory. Questions that ask about event-specific or person-specific information routinely fail to discover these personal meanings, because the questions do not match how the respondent has framed the information. For example, a question about labor union influence on a teacher's strike is likely to puzzle a respondent who focused only on the strike's impact on children.

Specific questions can confirm the presence or absence of specific knowledge. But they are too narrowly targeted to assess the full scope of an individual's knowledge about a particular situation. For instance, in July 2010, pollsters asked a national sample of Americans about the depth of the oil well that was then leaking in the Gulf of Mexico to gauge their attention to the disaster. Of the respondents, 49 percent did not know the answer (Pew Research Center, 2010a). But that did not warrant the conclusion that those who gave wrong answers were unfamiliar with the Gulf disaster or did not grasp its environmental, economic, social, and political significance.

Opinion instability poses another measuring problem. It is often misinterpreted as a sign that people's answers are mere guesses because they have not formed opinions about a particular situation. That interpretation ignores the fact that it is not uncommon for people to change their interpretation of meanings when later information presents different perspectives or seems to contradict earlier impressions. For example, when two airplanes crashed into the World Trade Center's Twin Towers in New York on September 11, 2001, many observers, including trained journalists, stored the information initially as a tragic airplane accident. But the widely understood meaning that emerged very quickly thereafter was that this was an intentional attack on the United States by terrorists based in the Middle East. During evolving situations—like political campaigns, weather disasters, or interpersonal relationships—meanings drawn from data often remain in flux indefinitely.

Finally, happenings take on different meanings when some people see them through rose-colored lenses and others see only doom and gloom. A 2010 nationwide poll that checked the public's knowledge about widely publicized recent news stories illustrates the optimist/pessimist dichotomy (Pew Research Center, 2010a). Responses to multiple-choice questions showed that 77 percent of the respondents knew that American-born children of illegal immigrants were American citizens, and 73 percent knew that Congress had passed health reform legislation in 2010. More than half were aware that General Petraeus was commanding U.S. forces in Afghanistan, that the national unemployment rate was 10 percent, and that a leaking oil well in Gulf waters was 5,000 feet below the surface. But instead of rejoicing about the knowledge displayed in these correct answers, most of the scholarly commentary bemoaned only the failures.

Critics complained about the low state of the public's political knowledge because a mere 19 percent of the respondents were aware that David Cameron was Britain's new Prime Minister, and only 28 percent knew that John Roberts was the Chief Justice of the U.S. Supreme Court. Barely a third (34 percent) knew that crucial economic relief legislation, the Troubled Asset Relief Program (TARP), was started during the George W. Bush, rather than the Barack Obama, administration.

The critics' dismay about these low numbers was intensified because the report showed that the public had paid more attention to trivial, nonpolitical information than to political fare. Of the respondents, 85 percent could identify Twitter as an information-sharing network, and 63 percent correctly identified South Africa as the host of the 2010 World Cup.

Validity of Fact-Based Knowledge Measures

And now to a caveat about complaints regarding the validity of fact-based knowledge as a civic IQ measure. Fact-based knowledge measures are quite good in assessing citizens' ability to memorize the facts deemed important by the questioner. Proponents of these tests also are correct when they claim that citizens who can spout factual data are likely to have high civic IQ scores. This holds true because high scores in tests about specifics identify political sophisticates who are exceptionally interested in particular areas of knowledge, often for personal or professional reasons. This passion for politics is usually the chief force that motivates detailed learning and conscious efforts to store these details in memory (Case, 2007).

At the upper end of the political knowledge scale, sophistication and a high civic IQ usually coincide, but at more average levels, citizens usually have limited knowledge of factual details, even when their political insights are keen. For the sake of accuracy, measurement of the civic IQ must therefore be based on measuring comprehension, rather than on recall of data points.

It is also true that factual knowledge does not necessarily equate to true insight and understanding of politics, just as intellectual brilliance does not necessarily equate to common sense. Sparsely educated residents in low-income neighborhoods routinely demonstrate greater political savvy about urban education and crime problems than do their better-educated peers in upper-class suburban neighborhoods (Graber, 2001). Many people, especially at younger ages, can recall facts verbatim without knowing what they mean. They may be able to recite the words of the national anthem flawlessly without knowing what it means to watch the national flag "gallantly streaming" over the "ramparts," and with no recall or conception of the "perilous fight" to which the lyrics refer.

Collective Public Opinion

The frequent findings of citizens' political ignorance are matched by less frequent, but also amply documented findings, that most people do pay attention to news and do form rational opinions about important public policy issues. Gaps in individual knowledge and understanding disappear when collective opinions are measured. The baseline research that supports the claim that collective public opinion is sound and in tune with the political needs of the country was done by political scientists Benjamin Page and Robert Shapiro and published in 1992. Since then, these findings have been confirmed by other scholars' research.

Page and Shapiro's main contention is based on a time-series analysis of polls about the merits of various U.S. foreign policies. The evidence confirms that public opinion is "rational, in the sense we have defined the term—real, stable, differentiated, consistent, coherent; reflective of basic values and beliefs; and responsive (in predictable and reasonable ways) to new information and changing circumstances." They concluded that "the public's preferences form coherent patterns that reflect underlying goals and values and beliefs" (Page and Shapiro, 1992). In sum, they concluded that the civic IQ is keen enough to allow American democracy to function properly.

In the wake of revolutionary changes in the volume and content of the news supply and in patterns of news consumption since 1992, does Page and Shapiro's diagnosis remain valid? Do citizens' answers to poll questions still indicate that they take note of new political information and that this information permits them to form reasonable opinions? Or is the opposite becoming true? Is it true that the news has deteriorated in a desperate struggle by mass media enterprises to retain audiences who prefer lightweight, entertaining stories to complex, hard news?

The decline in the public's use of traditional news sources has raised fears that many citizens may be flocking to inferior "new" media. They may be ignoring news altogether or picking up snippets of political information from various entertainment presentations, gaining little solid knowledge from the process. Teenagers who belong to the millennial generation have been called "the dumbest generation" by Mark Bauerlein, a professor at Emory University. He contends, and many others concur, that the new communication technologies are fostering a culture of narcissism, where citizens spend untold hours communicating with each other about trivial personal matters, ignoring happenings in the public sphere (Bauerlein, 2008).

How realistic are these fears? I chose to answer that question by checking the quality of citizens' answers when pollsters queried sample populations repeatedly in recent years about public policy issues that were in flux.

Polls as Indicators of Civic IQ Quality

My assistants and I scrutinized seven time series of public-opinion polls that covered important public-policy issues using the answers to poll questions as measures of citizens' attention to politics and indicators of the quality of the civic IQ. We concentrated on situations where public opinion had shifted dramatically—by more than 10 percentage points—during the early years of the twenty-first century when social networks had started their explosive growth, luring people away from older news sources.[1] We tried to ascertain whether these major changes in public opinion seemed reasoned or haphazard.

To explore likely explanations for shifts in public opinions, we also examined the political scene preceding the opinion changes. Were there mind-changing events, especially in the thrust of news stories in newspapers and nightly television newscasts in the weeks before the participants answered the poll questions?[2] We searched for news stories that were covered repeatedly on multiple days, because that would increase the likelihood that most respondents had actually encountered them. Repetitions of breaking news stories are common and help to embed the contents in the audiences' memories. Had the percentage of people with no opinions about the events declined over time?

In a number of instances, pollsters asked whether respondents were aware of issues, whether they had paid attention to relevant news stories, and how well they understood particular situations or were confused about them. We recorded these responses as well, to judge whether they confirmed our other findings. They did, in all cases.

Public-opinion pollsters seldom ask respondents for the specific reasons that prompted their answers, and it is only rarely possible and feasible to conduct post hoc interviews with these respondents to tap into their reasoning. Our claims about the rationality, if any, of particular opinions must therefore rely on reasonable inferences. We inferred that people had paid attention to news about political developments if their opinion changes made sense, considering news reports about substantial transformations of the political scene that were published two or more weeks prior to the polling dates. We deemed opinion changes thoughtful, even when policies in tune with these opinions ultimately proved to be wrong.

Inferential reasoning is always hazardous. However, if a large body of evidence drawn from diverse sources supports the inferences, the confidence level rises. This is why we tested the reasonableness of opinion changes in multiple important policy areas that satisfied our criteria: opinion changes amounting to at least 10 percentage points. Situations that satisfied these criteria were opinions about the following:

- Engaging in the Iraq war
- The merits of energy policies
- Civil liberty concerns raised by the Patriot Act
- Education issues surrounding the No Child Left Behind Act
- Investing Social Security funds in the stock market
- Adding prescription drugs to Medicare coverage
- Awareness of global warming issues

The findings for the first four issues are discussed at length in the following sections. They suffice to support our inferences. The findings for the other three issues are summarized after the in-depth discussions.

Iraq War Opinions

Among these seven issues, public opinion changes were most dramatic with respect to U.S. policy in Iraq. In response to the general question "Do you favor or oppose the U.S. war with Iraq?" there was a drop of 17 percent in favorable responses and a corresponding increase in unfavorable responses in the six-month period between April and October 2003. By June 2005, 20 months after the October poll, there was another 15 percent drop in those who favored the war with Iraq and a 16 percent increase in those who opposed it. Only a small number of respondents—2 to 3 percent—had no opinion. These results are shown in Table 1.1.

Table 1.1 Do you favor or oppose the U.S. war with Iraq?

	Favor %	Oppose %	No Opinion %
2003 Apr 22–23	71	26	3
2003 Oct 24–26	54	43	3
2005 Jun 16–19	39	59	2
2007 Jan 15–18	36	61	3

Excerpted from The Gallup Organization, "Gallup's Pulse of Democracy: The War in Iraq" (http://www.galluppoll.com/). Various dates, as noted.

Such low no-opinion percentages are common when pollsters ask about well-reported issues. The fact that people have opinions, and these opinions vary in tandem with positive and negative developments reported by the news media, supports our conclusion that people do pay attention to political information, and sizable numbers will change their views to adapt to the new environment.

What accounts for the sharp drop in approval of the Iraq war that Table 1.1 shows? A flood of negative stories that were widely reported by newspapers and television broadcasts is the answer.

The stories called attention to the fact that fighting in Iraq continued and casualties were rising, even though President Bush had declared on May 1, 2003, that the war had ended. Weapons inspectors could not find any of the weapons of mass destruction that had been the official justification for the war. By spring 2005, news stories reported that U.S. intelligence agencies had relied on questionable sources for their charges that the government of Iraq possessed weapons of mass destruction, and they had probably exaggerated the dangers that such weapons would pose. Congress held hearings, and members expressed doubts about the accuracy of the administration's claims. Meanwhile, casualties continued to rise, though they were never large considering the size of the U.S. forces involved in the Iraq war.

In sum, a war that had been declared won still continued. Casualties, though small, rose steadily. Polls showed that majorities of citizens considered war costs excessive in terms of loss of lives and dollars spent. Reports of overcharges and mismanagement by private contractors who were profiteering from the war enhanced the image that the United States was wasting its resources at a time when its own domestic economy was shrinking. News stories conveyed the impression that much of the evidence supporting the war decision actually was wrong and possibly deliberately distorted. The message was that invading Iraq had been an expensive mistake.

Given all these amply publicized facts, the marked drop in public approval of the war was reasonable. Even though the Republican administration clung to its initial claims. and people's evaluations tended to be in accord with their party allegiance, disapproval of the war extended increasingly across partisan lines.

Other polls[3] also showed that people were monitoring events closely enough to notice fluctuations in the war situation and change their responses accordingly. For example, when rating U.S. progress in the Iraq war on a two-point scale, bimonthly fluctuations exceeded 10 percentage points, in tune with the thrust of the news. March and May 2004 and January and March 2005 are good examples, as shown in Table 1.2.

In March 2004, stories and photos saturated the media about four U.S. soldiers "butchered" by Iraqis, and how their mutilated bodies were put on public display. Television news programs showed emotion-arousing pictures of servicemen killed in action, coffins arriving in the United States, antiwar demonstrations, and

Table 1.2 In general, how would you say things are going for the U.S. in Iraq: very well, moderately well, moderately badly, or very badly (choices were rotated)?

	Well %	Badly %	No Opinion %
2004 Mar 5–7	55	43	2
2004 May 2–4	37	62	1
2005 Jan 7–9	40	59	1
2005 Mar 18–20	52	45	3

Excerpted from The Gallup Organization "Gallup's Pulse of Democracy: The War in Iraq" (http://www.galluppoll.com/). Various dates, as noted. To enhance clarity, the categories Very Well and Moderately Well have been combined to Well, and the categories Moderately Badly and Very Badly have been combined to Badly.

destruction in Iraq. A touching hour-long television special about Iraqi orphans was featured repeatedly. It included sequences where youngsters told how their parents had been executed. The special produced an outpouring of donations from the American public, evidence that people were paying attention and responding. Disapproval of the war grew stronger.

Deadly bombings of civilians by antigovernment forces and military combat went on in an unbroken sequence in 2004, and U.S. and Iraqi casualties continued to mount. Then, on April 30, 2004, the media were saturated with stories and gruesome photos about scandalous behavior by American troops who worked at the large Abu Ghraib prison in Iraq. The revelation of mistreatment and torture of Iraqi prisoners conveyed the impression that the Bush administration and the military condoned torturing of prisoners.

On the good news side, boosting approval of the war, in January 2005, Iraqis elected a 275-seat National Assembly, followed in February by the selection of a prime minister from the majority party. It seemed that democracy had come to the torn nation. Stories and photos of these encouraging developments saturated the media. Yet on February 28, an attack by suicide bombers killed more than 100 people and reminded everyone that there were still major problems. The suicide attack was interpreted as the opposition's reaction to the election of the new government.

Energy Policy Opinions

Fluctuations in public approval of the government's energy policy show similar correspondence between public opinion and the thrust of news stories. From 2003 to 2007, there was a steady decrease in those who thought that President Bush was doing a good job of improving the nation's energy policy. Table 1.3 records how people responded to a key question.

The steady drop in approval can be linked to a number of events that the news media publicized extensively. In chronological order, the first event, in August 2003, was a massive blackout on the East Coast and in the upper Midwest that paralyzed those sections of the United States for several days. Besides widespread coverage

Table 1.3 Do you think George W. Bush is doing a good job or a poor job in handling the nation's energy policy?

	Good Job %	Poor Job %	Fair/Mixed %	Unsure %
2003 Mar 3–5	39	45	7	9
2004 Mar 8–11	34	51	8	7
2005 Mar 7–10	32	54	7	7
2006 Mar 13–16	25	63	7	5
2007 Mar 11–14	26	63	7	4

The Gallup Organization "Presidential Ratings–Issues Approval" (http://www.gallup.com/poll/1726/Presidential-Ratings-Issues-Approval.aspx) and "Energy" (http://www.gallup.com/poll/2167/Energy.aspx), March 11–14, 2007.

of this event, it initiated a blame game between Democrats and Republicans about who had neglected energy safety.

News stories suggested the possibility of foul play and reminded many people about the widely publicized Enron scandal that had led to blackouts in California two years earlier. Enron, a Houston-based energy company, had gone bankrupt following risky financial practices that it had concealed through false reports. In each case, the government had failed to detect major auditing frauds in reports submitted by Enron as well as other private companies.

The sensational news stories about acrimonious conflicts in Congress and major scandals in the private sector were bound to arouse people's attention if they were monitoring political news.

Beginning in 2003, gas prices also started to rise sharply. As Bob Slaughter, the President of the National Petrochemical and Refiners Association, put it, people know that "America's standard of living and overall economic health are closely linked to the need for adequate supplies of natural gas and other forms of energy at reasonable, market-based prices" (Ivanovich, 2005). Rumors that the high prices were caused by greedy speculators' manipulations made them seem unjustified and predatory. People felt that their economic welfare had been sabotaged. The rumors aroused public anger.

At the end of 2003, Congress started a prolonged debate about a new energy policy that would increase the nation's oil supply. The bill was very controversial, and the debate was acrimonious because it involved the issue of oil exploration in Alaska's Arctic National Wildlife Refuge. Television news pictures focused repeatedly on the beautiful pristine environment, including herds of caribou that would be put at risk by oil diggings. Various environmental lobbies staged repeated colorful demonstrations against the policy change, including mass protests throughout all parts of the United States during Earth Day events.

In 2005, Hurricane Katrina and Hurricane Rita destroyed oil refineries and drilling rigs. The devastation and its impact were widely covered in print, as well as on television. The pictures were dramatic. The responses recorded in Table 1.4 reflect the public's rising concerns about energy issues.

There is an almost 10 percentage point increase from 2003 to 2007 in respondents who think the energy situation is very serious, with the increase peaking in 2006, when respondents who deemed the situation very serious jumped to 41 percent. Again, the evidence supports the conclusion that there were solid reasons for the public to become increasingly concerned about energy policy and, as is common, blame the president for the lack of a resolution.

You might argue here and elsewhere that public opinion was responding to conditions that people were actually experiencing, rather than to the thrust of media coverage of the events. That argument rings true for some of the energy-related situations

Table 1.4 Now turning to the subject of energy, how serious would you say the energy situation is in the United States: very serious, fairly serious, or not at all serious?

	Very Serious %	Fairly Serious %	Not at All Serious %	Unsure %
2003 Mar 3–5	28	59	11	2
2004 Mar 8–11	29	57	12	2
2005 Mar 7–10	31	56	10	3
2006 Mar 13–16	41	51	7	1
2007 Mar 11–14	37	55	7	1

The Gallup Organization "Presidential Ratings–Issues Approval" (http://www.gallup.com/poll/1726/Presidential-Ratings-Issues-Approval.aspx), March 11–14, 2007.

reported earlier, such as the rise in gasoline prices. But it holds true only partially for the blackouts that people experienced only in the East and Midwest and for the fallout from Hurricane Katrina and Hurricane Rita. When it comes to energy policy debates in Congress and the proposals for new legislation, most people do not pay attention unless media coverage is prominent and ample. How media frame these stories, and how they position and emphasize them in print and audiovisual reports, largely determines whether large numbers of people will actually notice these events and form opinions about them. The quality of monitorial citizenship depends almost entirely on the quality of news media coverage.

Between March 2006 and March 2007, media coverage of energy issues decreased, especially on television, because no major energy policy-related events happened. Perceptions of the seriousness of the country's energy problems declined slightly, absent media alarms. Still, in accord with the concerns raised by earlier media coverage, people continued to rate energy problems as serious and to give low grades to the president's performance in this crucial policy area. That is further evidence of the close linkage between media attention to events and changes in public opinions.

Civil Liberties Opinions

Government intrusion on civil liberties became a significant issue following the terrorist attacks on the U.S. mainland on September 11, 2001. A little over a month after the strikes, the USA Patriot Act became the law of the land. It greatly expanded the government's powers to intrude on the civil liberties of U.S. citizens.

One week after the attack, a poll by the Pew Research Center found that 55 percent of the respondents believed that the "average person will have to give up some freedoms in order to prevent such attacks in the future" (Pew Research Center, 2001). However, as Table 1.5 shows, subsequent events rekindled the public's concern for protecting civil liberties.

Most of the substantial changes in the public opinion polls can be correlated with major news broadcasts on civil liberties topics. While civil liberties were not discussed every day following the 9/11

Table 1.5 Do you think the Bush administration has gone too far, has been about right, or has not gone far enough in restricting people's civil liberties in order to fight terrorism (choices were rotated)?

	Too Far %	About Right %	Not Far Enough %	Unsure %
2002 Jun 21–23 ^	11	60	25	4
2002 Sep 2–4 ^	15	55	26	4
2003 Aug 25–26 ^	21	55	19	5
2003 Nov 10–12 ^	28	48	21	3
2006 Jan 6–8	38	40	19	3
2006 May 12–13	41	34	19	6

^ Asked of a half sample.
Excerpted from The Gallup Organization, "Gallup's Pulse of Democracy: The Patriot Act and Civil Liberties" (http://www.galluppoll.com/). Various poll dates.

attacks, there are periods when news reports focused intensively on the Patriot Act, spying threats, and wiretaps. Oddly, the tone of nearly all the news broadcasts was negative in reports concerning the government's respect for civil liberties. There was little balance.

For example, when Congress debated renewal of the Patriot Act, news reports concentrated on the opponents' arguments while slighting the arguments of supporters. At the time, the polls indicated that the public was ambivalent about censorship issues, split between the desire to protect civil liberties and the willingness to trade privacy for greater safety from terrorism. These are the kinds of situations when the framing of poll questions and of news stories can easily determine public reactions, placing them on either side of the opinion divide.

The shift from privileging protection to privileging privacy is also clear from answers to the question shown in Table 1.6. The pattern was similar in numerous other polls that addressed the issue of civil liberties in general or dealt with specific topics, such as the privacy of international telephone conversations or e-mail.

As Table 1.6 shows, there was a 16 percentage point drop in support for essentially unrestrained government monitoring of private

Table 1.6 Which comes closer to your view: the government should take all steps necessary to prevent additional acts of terrorism in the U.S., even if it means your basic civil liberties would be violated, or the government should take steps to prevent additional acts of terrorism but not if those steps would violate your basic civil liberties (choices were rotated)?

	Take Steps, Even If Civil Liberties Violated %	Take Steps, But Not Violate Civil Liberties %	No Opinion %
2002 Jan 25–27	47	49	4
2002 Jun 21–23	40	56	4
2003 Nov 10–12	31	65	4
2005 Dec 16–18	31	65	4

Excerpted from Gallup polls in "The Polls—Trends: Privacy in the Information Age," *Public Opinion Quarterly* 70(3):375-401 by Samuel J. Best, Brian S. Krueger, and Jeffrey Ladewig (2006).

communications between January 2002 and November 2003, and a corresponding increase for prioritizing civil liberties over security concerns. Possible reasons include multiple reports about Justice Department misbehavior, including statistics about the number of complaints that had been filed against that department. The news media also featured stories about abuse charges leveled against other federal agencies for alleged violations of citizens' privacy. They included charges of rampant abuses by the Federal Bureau of Investigation (FBI), the Drug Enforcement Agency (DEA), and the Immigration and Naturalization Service (INS).

Coverage of civil liberties issues was also spurred in the fall of 2003, when the administration began to campaign for expansion of the Patriot Act. Attorney General Ashcroft went on a well-publicized promotion tour that spanned the entire country. From then on, stories about the alleged horrors produced by the Patriot Act flourished, with daily stories during some weeks. Sizable groups of citizens apparently took their cues from the media's condemnation of the act, even though other polls had shown that few citizens felt personally victimized by government spying or knew people who had been victimized.

The poll questions about civil liberties were raised initially because it became known that the Bush administration had monitored international calls and e-mail messages of American citizens without first seeking court orders, as required by law. The administration claimed that the president's war powers gave the executive branch the right to screen these messages without court permission. It also claimed that monitoring was essential to intercept messages conveyed by terrorists in pursuit of their illicit aims. The news media devoted a great deal of time and space to arguments that refuted the administration's claims. News stories avoided emphasis on security arguments. Public opinion changed in tune with the framing of the bulk of the news coverage.

Education Policy Opinions

Polling on education, specifically on the No Child Left Behind Act, presents some interesting features that shed additional light on the distinctions that people make when they form opinions that reflect their own situations. Realizing that people who have a personal stake in an issue may view it differently than people who do not, pollsters asked respondents whether or not they had children in school and separated the answers accordingly. The opinions of the two groups differ by as much as 9 percentage points on some scores, as shown in Table 1.7.

In 2007, when pollsters asked people how favorably or unfavorably they viewed the No Child Left Behind Act, which mandates periodic testing of students' basic skills, they also asked to what degree the respondents considered themselves knowledgeable about the law and its impact. Table 1.8 shows the results.

Not surprisingly, Table 1.8 shows increasing disapproval of the law from 2003 to 2007. Knowledgeable respondents were more disenchanted than people likely to have paid less attention to news about the No Child Left Behind Act.

Media coverage of the act in both print media and on television was predominantly negative. It pointed to harmful consequences, with little mention of the benefits that supporters of the law claimed. President Bush, for example, predicted that the act would

Table 1.7 In your opinion, is there too much emphasis on achievement testing in the public schools in this community, not enough emphasis on testing, or about the right amount?

	No Children in School				Public School Parents				
	'02 %	'04 %	'05 %	'06 %	'07 %	'02 %	'04 %	'05 %	'06 %	'07 %
Too Much Emphasis	30	30	35	36	41	32	36	39	45	52
Not Enough Emphasis	20	23	17	28	15	14	20	17	17	10
About the Right Amount	46	40	39	32	42	54	43	43	37	38
Don't Know	4	7	9	4	2	*	1	1	1	*

Excerpted from The 40th Annual PDK/Gallup Poll. June 12–29, 2007.

Table 1.8 From what you know or have heard about the No Child Left Behind Act, do you have a very favorable, somewhat favorable, somewhat unfavorable, or very unfavorable opinion of the Act—or don't you know enough about it to say?

| | National Totals | | | | | Know Great Deal/ Fair Amount |
	'03 %	'04 %	'05 %	'06 %	'07 %	'07 %
Very + Somewhat Favorable	18	24	28	32	31	38
Very Favorable	5	7	7	9	4	5
Somewhat Favorable	13	17	21	23	27	33
Somewhat Unfavorable	7	12	15	18	23	28
Very Unfavorable	6	8	12	13	17	27
Don't Know Enough to Say	69	55	45	37	29	7
Somewhat + Very Unfavorable	13	20	27	31	40	55
Don't Know	*	1	*	*	*	*

*Less than one-half of 1 percent.
Excerpted from The 40th Annual PDK/Gallup Poll, June 12–29, 2007.

close the gap in educational achievements between U.S. children and their peers in numerous other countries. He also talked about the importance of accountability in the public education system and the need to develop uniform tests.

On the negative side, news stories alleged that toughening of teacher licensing requirements had produced teacher shortages. Excessive attention on coaching students for tests slighted other areas of the curriculum, like history, art, and music. Disabled students and students for whom English was a second language were unduly burdened. Television showed pictures of children in classrooms—always an emotionally stirring sight—and featured experienced teachers who complained that the act was producing far more harm than good, and that the testing costs drained funds from more worthwhile programs. There were even claims that the act inspired corrupt behavior. The pressure to keep test scores high led some teachers to support or condone cheating. Some states refused to accept national mandates on education that overrode state authority. News stories also reported congressional concern and plans to revise the act, suggesting that all was not well.

The constant stream of news coverage shrank the number of citizens who said that they did not know enough about the No Child Left Behind Act to comment on it from a high of 69 percent in 2003 to a moderate 29 percent in 2007—a 40 percent drop. Obviously, people were paying attention and forming opinions. The balance between negative and positive views also changed between 2003 and 2007, with negative evaluations growing by 27 percentage points as people became more familiar with the act's impact. Positive evaluations grew as well, but only by 13 percent.

Again, as was true of the other case reports, it is reasonable to ascribe the changing responses in public-opinion polls to public attention to media coverage, and to credit the public with learning from the news and adjusting opinions accordingly.

That does not mean that every respondent changed. Because opinion changes are uncomfortable, many respondents most likely processed the news reports in ways that allowed them to keep their beliefs stable. Although we lack data on individual changes, a goodly proportion of citizens obviously switched their opinions, producing major changes in the distribution of opinions. The thrust of the changes matched prevailing news coverage.

Other Poll Results

The findings about proposed changes in Social Security funding, Medicare coverage, and global warming policies corroborate the four cases reported in detail in the previous sections.

The questions about Social Security asked whether it was a good or bad idea to allow individuals to invest a portion of their Social Security taxes on their own, whether the respondent would support or oppose such a plan, and whether the respondent favored or opposed a policy change. Parallel to news stories, opinions shifted from approval to disapproval.

The Medicare questions involved a new prescription drug plan initiated by the Bush administration. Respondents were asked whether they thought the program was working or not working "based on what you have read or heard." Because the plan was complex, pollsters questioned eligible adults whether they personally understood the plan very well, somewhat well, not too well, or not at all. They also asked whether respondents would join the plan. Media coverage focused on the complexity of the plan and became more negative over time. Correspondingly, the majority of senior citizens indicated that they did not understand the plan very well, that they doubted that it was working, and that they would not participate. Similar to news trends, opinions became more negative over time.

On global warming, the sharp rise in media coverage of the issue was reflected in a sharp increase in the numbers of respondents who said that they had heard "a lot" or "some" about the problem, and a sharp drop in the numbers of respondents who had heard "not much" or "nothing at all." When asked what they considered "the single biggest environmental problem facing the world," the percentage of respondents who listed global warming doubled in one year's time, from 16 percent to 33 percent. Their fear that global warming would pose a threat to them and their way of life also jumped by 10 percent over a ten-year span.

Conclusion

The seven cases confirm that Page and Shapiro's claims about the soundness of public opinions still hold, despite the drastic changes in news platforms and in audience-attention patterns. Apparently, the public still pays attention to important, widely covered problems, and a goodly portion of the public adjusts its opinions in line with the main thrust of media coverage.

Our content analyses showed that the arguments presented by the media and the supporting details supplied solid reasons for citizens to change their views in line with news framing of political developments. Such rational adjustments demonstrate that public-opinion processes continue to work well enough to assure the soundness of the collective civic IQ. In turn, the collective civic IQ could not be sound unless the majority of the individual opinions that it aggregates are sound. Assessments that average citizens know too little to have sound opinions about government are decidedly wrong when it comes to important, well-publicized political issues.

The evidence shows that, over time, the percentage of citizens who claim to be well informed about a problem rises and the number of citizens who have no opinion declines. That is another solid indicator of public attentiveness. It suggests that citizens may not pay attention to public-policy issues when they first arise, but when the issue continues to be in the limelight, they will note it and form opinions about it. There is also evidence that their knowledge broadens over time because learning is cumulative. The fact that positive and negative answers seem to be highly responsive to fluctuations of the favorableness of reported stories about a particular policy is additional evidence that citizens follow the news closely enough to keep track of the flow of political events.

The important overall conclusion of this chapter is that citizens' civic IQ, individually and collectively, is functioning adequately, despite scholars' damning verdicts. The public is not ignorant about essential political data and can form sound opinions, contributing to a reasonably well-functioning American democracy. The public still monitors the news about the political scene and responds to it. Democracy—government by the people—is still possible in the twenty-first century, if we define citizenship in ways that are realistic under contemporary conditions.

But what about the news media? Do they still supply enough solid political information so that citizens can monitor the political scene? Chapter Two addresses that question.

CHAPTER TWO
THE ADEQUACY OF THE NEWS SUPPLY

When it comes to adequacy of political news, American news media generally receive poor grades (Bennett et al., 2007; Jamieson, 2000; Pew Research Center 2006, 2007; Skocpol and Fiorina, 1999; Jones, 2009). Many critics blame ever-thinner coverage of essential political information for the public's ignorance about specific facts pertaining to public-policy realms.

In this chapter, we'll look at how well the media cover the range of issues in need of citizen surveillance. We'll also examine whether poll questions actually correspond to information that is available in the media.

What Do the News Media Actually Cover?

Because so many serious complaints about media performance are based on impressionistic appraisals of the news content, a massive systematic content analysis to investigate these allegations seemed in order. Therefore, I designed a study to ascertain the actual scope of public policy coverage and its usefulness for keeping citizens informed.[1]

The Research Design

The content analysis began in the summer of 2007 during a period that promised to be fairly ordinary, free from sensational events that might distort news patterns. To skirt regularities in coverage linked to specific days of the week—like featuring science news on Tuesdays and business news on Thursdays—we created a "constructed week" for the analysis. Accordingly, we analyzed news from consecutive weekdays over a period of five weeks. We omitted Saturday and Sunday coverage, because it serves different missions than regular weekday offerings, and also because many weekday audiences stay away from Sunday news.

For each day in the constructed week, we sampled political news from a broad array of sources to assess its usefulness for monitorial citizenship (introduced in Chapter One). Obviously, while individual news consumers cannot possibly tap into all sources of news in modern environments, collectively, citizens do draw information from a large number of diverse sources. Samples from these sources provide insights about the type of information that feeds public opinion about policy issues. We checked the following sources:

- Newspapers, including nationally and locally circulating papers
- Television, including local newscasts, network newscasts, cable newscasts, and evening talk shows
- Radio, including National Public Radio (NPR), all-news stations, brief newscasts on music stations, and syndicated radio talk programs
- Internet sources, which encompassed assorted liberal and conservative blogs.

For each of these sources, we recorded the political issues that were covered in the news on that day of the constructed week. We also judged the ease of making sense of the information presented by words and pictures. We noted whether the issues were merely outlined or covered in depth. We checked whether the discussion included sufficient context and multiple angles about a particular situation, without sacrificing clarity.

We rated messages as user-friendly if an eighth grader could grasp them as judged by popular reading-ease tests. User-friendliness of news stories is important because it affects the likelihood that audiences will pay attention to them.

Table 2.1 lists the news sources that we used for our content analysis. For the newspaper analysis, we concentrated on news stories, editorials, op-ed pieces, letters to the editor, and "news-in-brief" sections (which capsulize major news items treated at length elsewhere in the paper). For the television shows, we recorded half-hour programs, but stretched that to an hour for the 24-hour cable news channels. We recorded the cable news programs at the noon hour because audience attendance tends to peak then.

The array of news sources was selected to be "typical," which is an unreachable goal, of course. Nonetheless, even imperfect choices create a respectable, useful sample of the kinds of stories likely to be offered by news outlets. It is an even tougher challenge to select criteria for judging what citizens need to know, and *can* know, to perform their citizenship functions.

As explained in Chapter One, we used the criteria suggested by Michael Schudson's conceptualization of the duties performed by monitorial citizens (Schudson, 1998). They "should be informed enough and alert enough to identify danger to their personal good and danger to the public good. When such danger appears on the horizon, they should have the resources ... to jump into the fray and make a lot of noise" (Schudson, 1999: p. 23). In line with Schudson's reasoning, we evaluated the news published during our analysis in terms of the individual and collective dangers posed by the reported situations. Although we recorded and analyzed all stories in our sample, our analysis focused primarily on stories that presented an opportunity for public commentary or action.

To be included in the final tally, it needed to be obvious from reading the entire story that the subject involved a public-policy matter of concern for most Americans and required important decisions by political leaders. Citizens would therefore need to be

Table 2.1 News Sources for Content Analysis

Media	Examples	Frequency
Newspapers		
National papers	*The New York Times, The Wall Street Journal, Financial Times*	One paper daily
Local papers	*Chicago Tribune, Chicago Sun-Times*	One paper daily
Television		
National news	ABC, CBS, NBC	One 30-minute show daily
Local news	ABC, CBS, NBC affiliates	One 30-minute show daily
Cable news	CNN, MSNBC, Fox	One 60-minute noon show daily
News magazines: Morning shows, talk shows, etc.	*Larry King Live, Dateline NBC, BBC Newshour, Hannity & Colmes, Studio B with Shepard Smith*	One show daily
Radio		
Nationally syndicated programs	NPR programming, *The Rush Limbaugh Show,* local talk radio	One show daily
Blogs		
A-list blogs: As classified by political scientist Kevin Wallsten (2007)	Talking Points, Michelle Malkin, Daily Dish, America, Atrios, J-Walk, War and Piece, Hot Air	One liberal blog and one conservative blog daily

informed about the situation and would want their political leaders to pay heed to their concerns. The content analysis showed that these stories, for the most part, involved situations in which political leaders were likely to be sensitive to public opinions, especially in an election year.

For example, On August 1, 2007, the *Wall Street Journal* reported a story about production factors that contribute to high oil and gasoline costs, but are potentially changeable. On the same day, the *Chicago Tribune* presented data showing that the Veterans Administration often ignored symptoms of service-related mental problems in battle-scarred veterans. NPR had a story about Federal Emergency Management Agency (FEMA) trailers distributed in post-Katrina New Orleans, which were unlikely to survive a major new hurricane. The Daily Dish blog covered prospective presidential candidate Fred Thompson's recommendations for U.S. policies related to climate change. All of these stories were judged "citizenship relevant" because they warranted government action that might be influenced by citizens' pleas.

Stories that did not qualify as citizenship-relevant news because they lacked Schudson's elements of "danger to the public good" included multiple reports about candidate rankings in the presidential horse race. Likewise, we excluded stories about the sale of the Dow Jones & Company to media tycoon Rupert Murdoch, the passage of the lobbying-reform bill by the House of Representatives, and accounts of tensions between Ethiopia and Eritrea.

Predictions about the likely concerns of large sections of the public are always risky. However, in this case, reporters working for different news media shared them, buttressing our estimates about the kinds of stories that deserved the public's attention Reporters selected stories from a large pool of available news that might interest many, if not all, of their audience members. Given the roughly 200 stories in our news pool, it was tempting to compose an ideal daily "must-tell" list of news stories, and judge the wisdom of the journalists' choices in light of that list. We resisted that temptation because it is clear that there are solid arguments to buttress diverse choices. Fortunately, priorities differ.

The Context for Judging News Adequacy

Our judgment of the adequacy of the news supply involved two important considerations that are often ignored by researchers. One is the memory factor. The second consideration relates to the importance of specialization, or division of labor, that is unavoidable in large, complex organizations.

Memory Factors

Most judgments of the adequacy of the news supply for satisfying citizens' civic needs treat the content of news messages as if it were a lone stimulus administered to blank minds. In fact, the vast majority of important political topics that news media publish are familiar to news audience because a similar situation has arisen many times in the past.

Stories about presidential elections, unrest in the Middle East, or the public-health dangers linked to tobacco smoke are examples. The details of the stories will vary over time. Each election brings new sets of candidates, new episodes of violence in the Middle East, and new health-science advances. But the basic messages are the same. That means that news audiences can greatly enrich sparse messages about the most recent episode with details drawn from memories of past episodes.

People also store their evaluations of these events, the event history, and the linkages of the key event to other situations. The availability of this rich treasure of previously processed news for fleshing out incoming news can make even brief messages about ongoing events very meaningful. Therefore, most of the time, monitorial citizens will be adequately served by brief messages that alert them to important evolving situations.

Of course, there is always the danger that the facts from the past will not pertain to the current situation or that audience members will employ the wrong analogies. The consequences of such misinterpretations can be serious.

Specialization

Complex societies, such as modern states, cannot function without specialization. Members of legislative bodies, for example, divide legislative tasks and delegate them to small committees, which can then develop expertise in diverse realms, such as energy policy or the criminal justice system.

Similarly, citizens can focus their attention on only a limited array of issues, and their news media may serve them quite well with respect to these issues. Citizens who use other media will cover other policy areas. The total fund of information that the public gathers from all the media that citizens use is apt to reflect a broad spectrum of major political issues and perspectives.

The Adequacy of the News Diet

Some people rely heavily on newspapers for their political information; others rely primarily on over-the-air or cable television for political news; still others limit their news diet largely to blogs and Internet sources beyond the mainstream news platforms. To gain a complete picture of the news reaching the U.S. public, we examined all these sources. The discussions that follow focus on the overall adequacy of the news diet, as well as the adequacy for audiences who rely primarily on the print press, on broadcast news, or on Internet sources.

News Selection Issues

On most of our news analysis days, every news source provided two to ten stories of national importance that would be likely to concern monitorial citizens. These stories constituted only a fraction of the total political news, as Table 2.2 shows. This differentiation is important because monitorial citizens do not need to pay attention to all political news they encounter. Only a fraction of it requires close scrutiny.

The proportion of citizen-relevant news to total political news was highest on average for national television at 35 percent, and lowest for local television at 13 percent. The average proportion was 23 percent, so that just under one-quarter of available news stories involved matters warranting the monitorial citizen's attention and possible action. While individual citizens would find it difficult to cope with that load in its totality, specialization makes it manageable, because different citizens attend to different issues. In a nation with millions of citizens, it would be highly unusual if any widely covered issue escaped sizable public attention.

**Table 2.2 Average Proportion of Citizenship News
in Various News Sources**

News Sources	#	%	Overlap %
National paper	9	22	100
Local paper	6	17	23
24/7 cable	4	24	14
Local TV	2	13	0
National TV	3	35	9
Special host shows	4	25	17
Radio news	3	20	8
Blog, liberal	5	27	17
Blog, conservative	4	27	15

\# = average daily number of citizenship-relevant news stories;
% = percentage of total daily political news stories;
overlap = percentage of stories shared with national newspaper.

The possibility of specialization is enhanced by the diversity of the news focus in various news platforms. On average, only 13 percent of the news events reported by a national newspaper like the *New York Times* are also reported by other news sources. In turn, these other news platforms carry citizenship-relevant news stories that are missing from the *Times*. As mentioned, there is no ideal news diet.

News selection varies depending on the preferences of reporters, their editors, and their news audiences. Obviously, there is a huge gap between what all news sources combined actually covered during our analysis period and what they could have covered if they complied with the *New York Times* slogan of "All the News That's Fit to Print."

The columns in Table 2.2 show the following:

- The first column lists the average number of daily citizenship-relevant news stories in various news venues. The column shows that all news platforms offered a daily diet of citizenship-relevant stories. Newspapers were the richest, followed by blogs.
- The second column shows that citizenship-relevant news represents only a small portion of the total number of political

news stories. National television takes the lead, with fully 35 percent of its stories covering news essential for monitorial citizens.

- The third column reports the percentage of overlap with the New York Times, which is widely regarded as the preeminent supplier of U.S. political news. It is also the most widely used standard in studies of news impact.

Considering that our database does not cover all the news that is available to Americans on each day in multiple years, Table 2.2 should be treated as a blueprint of major features, rather than as an exact portrait of the news scene at a particular time. Table 2.3 provides the data on a weekly basis.

Citizenship-relevant news coverage tends to shrink during major crises, like weather disasters, scandals involving political elites, or sensational announcements in major political campaigns. For example, when we analyzed news output on August 17, 2007, we found that CNN had devoted 23 minutes to a live broadcast of rescue efforts in a mine disaster in Utah, slighting other news. The incident illustrates how news important for the monitorial citizen, like stories about the housing mortgage crisis facing millions of citizens, is periodically driven out by less far-reaching, but more immediately dramatic, events.

Locally oriented media, like local television news or the tabloid *Chicago Sun-Times,* sacrifice attention to national news in favor of covering local news. That does not mean that their coverage of essential civic information deserves to be condemned as inadequate, as has often been the case. Many local news stories are very salient to monitorial citizens who need to be attuned to local politics as well as national politics. In fact, for many citizens, local events are of greater immediate concern and impact than many national happenings. Besides, opportunities for influencing public policies locally are more abundant. For example, during our analysis period, the *Chicago Sun-Times* informed its readers about Illinois property taxes, rising electricity rates, a statewide ban on smoking tobacco, prohibition on strikes by teachers, and major changes in teen driving laws.

Table 2.3 Weekly Proportion of Citizenship News in Various News Sources

News Sources	Week 1 7-24-07			Week 2 8-1-07			Week 3 8-9-07			Week 4 8-17-07			Week 5 8-20-07		
	#	%	Overlap	#	%	Overlap	#	%	Overlap	#	%	Overlap	#	%	Overlap
National paper	10	26	100	8	21	100	9	28	100	9	29	100	10	24	100
Local paper	7	14	50	6	20	0	3	7	22	10	29	33	6	13	10
24/7 cable	7	41	30	4	25	12	3	18	22	1	4	0	5	31	4
Local TV	4	25	0	1	6	0	2	13	0	1	7	0	2	12	0
National TV	3	30	0	4	44	12	4	44	22	3	42	11	1	14	0
Special host shows	9	30	30	1	12	0	4	26	22	2	28	11	3	30	20
Radio news	2	20	20	4	16	0	4	44	11	2	8	0	3	11	10
Blog, liberal	4	18	20	2	28	12	5	16	22	6	37	11	8	36	20
Blog, conservative	4	33	20	3	23	12	1	11	11	7	36	22	4	33	10

= Average daily number of citizenship-relevant news stories; % = percentage of total daily political news stories; overlap = percentage of stories shared with national newspaper.

News Diversity

On average, 23 different topics were covered by our sample of news sources each day, with a daily-topic range from 19 to 26. Table 2.4 lists the topics for each of our sample days.

Table 2.4 Citizenship-Relevant News Topics*

Date	Topic Ranking	Topic
Tuesday, July 24	1	New Orleans problems
	2	Iraq war
	3	Charter school politics
	4	Tax breaks for big business
	5	Violence in Pakistan
	6	Federal budget
	7	Presidential campaign
	8	Plastic bag ban
	9	China imports safety
	10	Low pay scales for part-time workers
	11	Diet soda health risk
	12	Smoking problems
	13	Seat belts on school buses
	14	U.S. Attorney questioned by Congress
	15	Air travel security
	16	Minimum wage
	17	Floods in U.S.
	18	Obesity problems
	19	Housing market problems
	20	Medical care quality
	21	Air traffic controllers
	22	Immigrant issues
	23	Al Qaeda
	24	Impeach Bush movement
Wednesday, August 1	1	Problems in mortgage market
	2	Inflation danger
	3	Oil prices

Table 2.4 (continued)

Date	Topic Ranking	Topic
	4	FDA food inspection
	5	Women's workplace discrimination
	6	Presidential campaign
	7	Unsafe China imports
	8	Rising restaurant meal costs
	9	Congress lobby reforms
	10	Concealment of government's antispy program
	11	Child abuse in soldier families
	12	Iraq war
	13	Attorney General Gonzalez's fate
	14	Care of mentally ill veterans
	15	Economic instability
	16	Ban of cell phones and MP3 players in high schools
	17	Campaign for Senate
	18	Cover-up of friendly fire incident
	19	Housing foreclosures
	20	iPod theft problem
	21	Unsafe FEMA trailers
	22	Climate change
Thursday, August 9	1	Housing crisis
	2	Peace plans for Korean peninsula
	3	China increases food export safety
	4	Immigration laws
	5	Government bailout of sagging economy
	6	Rise in food prices
	7	Fate of Guantanamo detainees
	8	Presidential campaign
	9	Iraq war
	10	CIA failures
	11	Safety of bridge construction
	12	Housing mortgage crisis
	13	Immigration issues
	14	Medical benefits for seniors
	15	Credit crisis

Table 2.4 (continued)

Date	Topic Ranking	Topic
	16	Attorney General Gonzalez's fate
	17	Torture
	18	U.S. role in Kosovo independence
	19	U.S. complaints about Iran
Friday,	1	Housing mortgage crisis
August 17	2	Worldwide economic declines
	3	Presidential campaign
	4	Credit crisis
	5	Terrorism: Padilla case
	6	Iran punitive policies
	7	Dangerous toy imports from China
	8	Use of DDT to control mosquitoes
	9	Safety of bridge construction
	10	Bush insiders problems: Karl Rove, Donald Rumsfeld
	11	Fallout from House Speaker Hastert resignation
	12	Healthful school cafeteria food
	13	Attorney General Gonzalez's troubles
	14	Iraq war issues
	15	Pakistan aiding Taliban in Afghanistan
	16	North Korea nuclear disarmament
	17	Employee health plans
	18	News media bias
	19	Cut in Federal Reserve discount rate to stimulate economy
	20	Unsafe toy imports from China
	21	Racial unrest in high schools
	22	Obesity problems
	23	Wiretapping/privacy issues
	24	New Orleans politics
	25	Immigration
	26	Global warming

Table 2.4 (continued)

Date	Topic Ranking	Topic
Monday, August 20	1	Diabetes epidemic
	2	Housing mortgage crisis
	3	Iraq war
	4	Afghanistan war
	5	Aftermath of VA Tech student shooting
	6	Legal defense for death row prisoners
	7	Presidential campaign
	8	Bush administration insider Karl Rove
	9	Mining regulation adequacy
	10	Energy conservation
	11	Immigration issues
	12	Rising cost of birth control
	13	Abu Ghraib trials of U.S. soldiers
	14	Faulty trans-fat labeling
	15	Farm subsidies
	16	Unsafe Chinese import toys
	17	Global warming
	18	Corruption in Congress
	19	Blog quality as news sources
	20	Attorney General Gonzalez, troubles
	21	Iraq war
	22	Wiretapping/privacy issues
	23	Value of congressional junkets abroad
	24	Terrorist organizations
	25	Public-safety issues during hurricanes

*Entries are for 2007 and may represent multiple stories about the same topic.

The diversity of news topics reflected in Table 2.4 is heartening because it means that the public can monitor a broad range of topics. The following list shows the 12 topics from the summer of 2007, arranged in the order of frequency of coverage, that were most widely reported during our analysis period. Many of them received attention in multiple stories that reported a wealth of detail. One might call these widely and amply covered topics a "national agenda," in the sense that they reached a very broad array of U.S. media audiences, regardless of their particular choice of news platforms. The availability of shared information in important policy areas reduces the risk that the nation will fragment into myriads of exclusive communication ghettoes.

1. Iraq war
2. Presidential campaign
3. Housing market problems
4. Iran's Middle East policies
5. New Orleans post-hurricane reconstruction
6. Immigration issues
7. Military incident cover-up
8. Federal budget woes
9. Plastic bag ban
10. Attorney General Gonzales hearings
11. Federal Reserve stimuli
12. Bush insider Karl Rove

User-Friendliness

Our analysis of the user-friendliness of news stories revealed that four out of five were easy to comprehend. Though not ideal, that is a decent comprehensibility score. Occasionally, stories rich in detail—which is most characteristic for newspapers—are confusing because people find it difficult to sort out the various strands of the story.

In fact, the subject matter of some stories is so complex that it is well-nigh impossible for news outlets to make them comprehensible to audiences who lack expertise. That happens most often with international stories or stories dealing with economic issues.

But by far, the most common problem is the reverse of complexity. News stories, even in newspapers, are often disturbingly short on detail. Most of them "tell the truth, but not the whole truth." Essential facts are often omitted or published earlier but not repeated, leaving audiences confused because they may not have seen these facts earlier or might not remember them.

Of course, much of the detail essential for understanding a story may already be stored in the news consumer's memory or may be extracted from later versions of the story. For instance, when a major bridge collapsed in Minnesota in 2007, killing more than a dozen people and injuring hundreds more, the news media covered the story repeatedly over several days. Each update added new background information in addition to reporting new developments. News consumers could also draw on their memory of other transportation disasters to fill in details missing from the coverage of the Minnesota event.

Fleshing out scant news reports is usually fairly easy for newspaper readers because many newspapers offer brief summaries of stories that help readers decide which of them merit reading in more extended versions in the same issue. Many blogs also help their audiences with news choices by providing news capsules. For example, the Hot Air blog features a Headlines section with the slogan "We Pick, You Click," reminding viewers that they can choose favorite items from the menu with a simple click of the mouse.

Choosing preferred stories and skipping others is more difficult for broadcast news audiences, despite the frequent announcements about upcoming stories. The audience does not know the precise time when particular stories will air, so is forced to stay tuned throughout the broadcast to catch desired items.

Variations in Specific News Venues

An overall analysis of citizenship-relevant news provides the big picture, but it blurs crucial details. With a burgeoning number of news platforms, fewer and fewer citizens sample all types. Therefore, it is important to look separately at the various types of news platforms—newspapers, television, and blogs—and judge how well they serve citizens' political needs in terms of both richness and user-friendliness of content.

Newspapers

Newspaper-reliant audiences are the most richly served group, both in numbers of citizenship-relevant stories and in the amount of detail made available to them about national and local issues. That was true for every daily sample covered by our content analysis. However, the richness of story details was often a mixed blessing. Depending on the state of readers' memories and their information-processing skills, ample story detail could clarify the picture or it could confuse readers and therefore discourage them from engaging with the topic. Confusion is especially common when papers present clashing views about the merits of a particular situation without providing readers with guidelines for making their own evaluations.

As mentioned, newspapers make it easy for readers to choose topics when they supply capsule versions of major stories, place them on front pages, and give them big headlines. But, judging from our sample, they still repeatedly miss reporting important situations where input of citizens' opinions could be crucial. Blogs and 24-hour cable news do a superior job of alerting citizens to a broad range of politically vital news, albeit often in headline formats that carry few details.

Television

Our study shows that, on balance, 24-hour cable outlets best serve the civic needs of their audiences. Given the lengthy time that these channels are on the air, and their extended headline service presentation style, cable outlets cover a broader span of citizen-relevant news than other types of news sources. Broadcasts are repeated throughout the day and night, increasing the chance that viewers will catch relevant news, often more than once.

Citizens who watch national television can find a menu of important national and international stories. Local television supplies important local news. However, though local news does provide important local coverage, public-policy news is comparatively sparse. Weather, crime, and sports get the lion's share of attention.

The main advantages of televised news are its audiovisual format, which simplifies information processing, coupled with its brevity, which keeps the costs of information acquisition to a minimum. The pictures add important dimensions and insights that are largely missing from printed news. The main disadvantage of televised news is excessive brevity, including slighting of essential background and contextual information that is missing from the pictures.

Blogs

Blogs are a strange breed of news. Reading simply what appears on the screen provides very little citizen-relevant information, even when it covers topics ignored by most mainstream media. However, the information offering increases exponentially when you consider that blogs usually provide clickable links to additional information. That opportunity gives willing audience members a chance to explore preferred topics in great depth. The links lead to nontraditional as well as traditional media.

While the information that blogs offer is often unabashedly partisan, violating hallowed norms of objectivity, blogs may report dozens and even hundreds of comments about their messages, giving citizens access to a broad array of views. Bloggers may also encourage political participation by asking their audiences for additional information or for help in interpreting a story. This is quite different from traditional media, which claim to offer expert information and, until very recently, have not generally solicited audience input.

In sum, when it comes to feeding the civic IQ, mature audiences endowed with memories stored over lifetimes of varying length receive sufficient information to perform their civic functions adequately at the national level. All of the news venues analyzed here provided alarm bells to alert interested citizens when major public policies were ripe for the national political agenda. However, all too often, the available information was too sketchy to fully judge the significance of the situation, even considering that it supplemented information stored in citizens' memories.

Still, the news supply that we examined under our research microscope was generally rich enough to arouse citizens' concerns about important political issues. This positive judgment about the adequacy of the news media's performance of civic duties is by no means unqualified, but it deserves enormous respect nonetheless. Our discussion now turns to the most serious qualifications.

Realistic Expectations about News Media Performance

In Chapter One, I argued against judging citizens from an idealistic rather than a realistic perspective. The same considerations are important when judging the performance of the news media. Ideally, the news media are a vital part of democratic governance because they supply citizens with information those citizens need to monitor their government. Therefore, news media should make citizens' political education their highest priority. The reality is quite different.

Economic Constraints

American news media are privately owned, profit-oriented enterprises. Traditionally, their main income has come from selling advertising space to customers who want access to media audiences to hawk their products and causes.

The necessity to keep profits high by attracting big audiences compels news media to feature stories that are likely to capture and hold the attention of large, heterogeneous groups of people. That pressure leads to excesses of hyped, often negative journalism. It also explains why much of the news has become less objective and more ideological. Seemingly irreconcilable conflicts are far more exciting than situations where all parties receive both blame and credit. The current news-story style runs counter to the ideal that news should be as measured as possible and commentary should be clearly identified.

Audience data also shows that the public is not primarily attracted to news that has broad political significance. Most of the time, people prefer news that is useful for daily life. News providers increasingly try to honor such preferences, because competition for audiences has been escalating steadily, thanks to the mushrooming of readily accessible news venues in the United States and elsewhere. All compete with each other for the same limited set of human eyeballs. When audiences are given multiple choices, they tend to splinter into smaller groups.

Smaller audiences mean shrinking resources for news providers, because advertising fees are geared to audience sizes. Lower advertising fees translate into lower profits. Shrinking profit margins in individual enterprises have forced cutbacks in staff; these cutbacks put additional workloads on the remaining employees. Fewer reporters with fewer resources at the mainstream media equate to fewer news stories and a focus on simple stories, cheaply gathered close to home. On round-the-clock media, like cable television, the pressure to provide news on a 24-hour, 7-day schedule also encourages resorting to easily gathered fluff pieces. Internet search engines are portals to a wealth of up-to-date important political information that could enrich the content of news stories.

The traditional media find their news turf eroded by the new media's ability to publish breaking stories instantly. That forces these prime sources of news to abandon the lure of featuring freshly breaking stories and attract audiences in other ways. But when they turn to more analytical and interpretive reporting, they are likely to trespass into the turf of editorial commentary. That creates the impression that news stories are politically biased, undermining the media's credibility and the public's trust in news sources.

Journalism Norms

Other constraints on news production arise from hallowed journalistic values and conventions. For example, journalists love "scoops." They want to be the first to publish important stories.

The zeal to rush to publication with breaking news fosters mistakes and misinterpretations. The *beat system,* under which journalists routinely cover news-rich locations like the governor's office or the police station, privileges news from customary locations over news that happens elsewhere. *Pack journalism,* born from the desire to match competitors' coverage of important topics, homogenizes criteria for news selection so that different media become rivals in conformity.

Citizen Journalism

The emergence of nonprofessional citizen journalism is praiseworthy from the perspective of increasing the number of voices in the public sphere. But from a quality perspective, it has potentially serious drawbacks. Most citizen reporters who blog about political issues lack training in selecting and covering newsworthy events, and identifying and analyzing their most essential features. They lack the writing and reasoning skills that are required for clear and concise reporting. Many of their stories are little more than responses to comments by randomly chosen members of the audience (Pew Research Center, 2008a).

Stories reported by nonprofessionals tend to concentrate on trivial local news and social events in their neighborhoods. Unlike professional journalists, citizen journalists seldom tackle complicated political issues. They rarely conduct systematic research. We can disagree about the respective merits of professional and nonprofessional reporting, but if clear delineation of information about complex political issues is important in a democracy, citizen journalists, as a group, are a poor substitute for their professional counterparts.

It is also important to keep in mind that the collective noun *news media* refers to a broad range of institutions. It includes newspapers, news magazines, television, radio, and the Internet. It also refers to individual news outlets within these broad categories. There is a wide gulf between the rich menu of global news offered by the *New York Times* and the fare offered by scores of tabloids and small-town newspapers that highlight local society news. U.S. media contain much journalistic wheat along with generous portions of chaff, and the proportions vary widely in individual news outlets. Fortunately, any citizen willing to make the effort can find essential current information more readily in the twenty-first century than ever before (Entman, 2005).

When judging the performance of news sources, we also must keep in mind that no news source—not even a large print medium that devotes most of its news hole to political stories—can report "All the News That's Fit to Print." However, as shown by our content analysis, collectively, U.S. news media are capable of covering a large slice of important news in timely fashion while such knowledge is useful, or even essential, for political action.

The Impact of Waning Credibility

The conclusion that, despite its shortcomings, the news supply is adequate for forming serviceable public opinions does not mean that individual citizens are or should be satisfied with the slice of news made available to them. For instance, I have noted the scarcity of public-policy news on local television broadcasts. I have also pointed out the thinness of many stories and the puzzles created by presenting clashing points of views. The picture becomes even bleaker when you consider that the public discounts news stories because of the waning credibility of all types of news media.

Declining trust shrinks the influence of the news media on the public's thinking. It diminishes the value of excellent reporting. Disdain for the news springs from people's own appraisals, the general climate of distrust of politics and politicians, and the many stories on the Internet and elsewhere that attack the credibility of public figures and question the accuracy of news.

Between 1998 and 2008, for example, the percentage of people who believe "all or most" of what news organizations publish dropped from 42 to 30 percent for CNN, from 30 percent to 24 percent for NBC and ABC national news, and from 28 to 22 percent for CBS News. Of the audience, 9 to 12 percent believed nothing that was broadcast on these platforms (Pew Research Center, 2008a). Although the drop is not dramatic, it is nonetheless shocking, because credibility was already disturbingly low before 2008 when this survey was taken.

Large portions of the audience also believe that stories are often inaccurate, and that journalists do not care about the people whose stories they report and do not feature the stories that are of greatest interest to their audiences. Furthermore, audiences regard the news media as politically biased (Pew Research Center, 2008a).

Audience reactions to news media coverage must be kept in historical perspective. As mentioned, at the start of the twenty-first century, regard for most major institutions in the United States and elsewhere was at low ebb. Still, when people were asked in 2008 how much they enjoyed keeping up with the news, only 15 percent confessed to little or no enjoyment (Pew Research Center, 2008b).

History also shows that politicians and the general public are fickle and schizoid in their condemnations as well as their praise. The founders of our nation were the first to carp about its venal, lying press on the one hand, and on the other hand, the first to agree that, warts and all, it was the bedrock on which democratic freedoms rest.

Mismatches Between News Supply and Poll Questions

If news coverage is adequate and people do pay attention to it despite their skepticism about the accuracy of the news, why do they have so much trouble answering social scientists' knowledge test questions? Chapter One discussed the difficulty of matching poll questions to the ways in which people actually record information in memory. Here, we look at another issue that distorts knowledge score: an insufficient match between the questions that pollsters ask and the information that the news media supply to the respondents.

Obviously, people cannot answer questions correctly if they did not receive the targeted information required or if the answer requires overly complex calculations. In short, knowledge questions that ignore the information supply available to respondents are poor gauges of the respondent's political IQ.

To shed some light on these measurement issues, my assistants and I investigated a number of situations where citizens' wrong answers to poll questions had given rise to charges of rampant political ignorance. How well had the information requested by pollsters matched the readily available news media information supply in the weeks and months preceding the polling dates? How parallel were the main themes and frames in news stories to the main themes and frames tapped by poll questions?

The disjuncture between poll questions posed to Americans and the knowledge base readily available to answer them emerges exceptionally clearly from an analysis of the public's knowledge about President Ronald Reagan's policies. My study of the Reagan polls was inspired by an article by renowned University of California, Los Angeles (UCLA) political science professor Martin Gilens, published in the *American Political Science Review* under the title "Political Ignorance and Collective Policy Preferences" (Gilens, 2001). Among other issues, Gilens noted that a national sample of American citizens could not answer questions posed in a survey by the National Election Studies (NES) in 1988 about various policies of the outgoing Reagan administration.

The Reagan Polls

Gilens's study focused, in part, on three questions (Gilens, 2001: p. 380):

- Have federal efforts to improve and protect the environment increased, decreased, or stayed about the same as they were in 1980, at the start of the Reagan administration?
- Compared to 1980, has the federal budget deficit gotten smaller, stayed about the same, or gotten larger?
- Compared to 1980, has the level of unemployment in the country gotten better, stayed about the same, or gotten worse?

Did the media supply the information required to answer these questions? And, more important, were the knowledge and the calculations required to make these comparisons reasonable indicators of the kind of civic knowledge that average Americans should have and that the media should therefore address?

Let's first look at the match between the questions asked by the NES and the information supplied by the news media. To answer the poll questions, the respondents would need to remember, or be reminded about, what conditions prevailed eight years earlier at the start of the Reagan administration in 1980. What efforts "to improve and protect the environment" (whatever that might mean) were then underway? What was the federal deficit in 1980, and what was the 1980 unemployment level?

Secondly, the respondents would need to be able to compare 1988 environmental improvement efforts to similar efforts eight to ten years earlier, using unspecified yardsticks. For example, effects might be judged in terms of breadth of impact, novelty, or budget allocations. Respondents would also need to know the size of the 1988 federal budget deficit and the 1988 unemployment figures.

The correct answers to the NES questions were that federal efforts to improve the environment declined during the Reagan years, measured by spending figures, legislative changes, or environmental policy enforcement. The federal deficit increased numerically and in real terms. And, according to the Bureau of Labor Statistics, unemployment dropped from 7.5 percent to 5.4 percent.

Aside from specialists and aficionados in these policy areas, most adult Americans would be unlikely to have this information at their fingertips in 1988. In the real world of American politics, average citizens cannot be expected to remember data in three specific policy realms spanning two presidential terms, or to do their own calculations to compare conditions at the start and the end of an eight-year administration.

If such data is important, the mass media should have refreshed citizens' knowledge periodically, and especially at the end of Reagan's presidential term when election campaigns were in progress and citizens needed to assess the incumbent's performance. Did the news media do the job? Our research shows that they did so, but only in part.

Television Offerings

My assistants and I checked the Vanderbilt television broadcast archives for 1988 news broadcasts of stories covering environmental protection, the federal budget deficit, and unemployment. To ascertain that all hits were valid, we performed key-word searches on the extended abstract versions available in the daily broadcast reports. We found that all three networks did, indeed, cover all of the issues in 1988, though rarely in the most prominent sections of the newscasts and with only moderate time allotments—generally two minutes or less.

If audiences paid attention, they should have found it easiest to answer questions about the budget deficit. In 1988, ABC nightly news covered the topic explicitly five times, CBS covered it six times, and NBC covered it eight times. The stories ranged from factual presentations about the size of the deficit to analytical pieces about its various economic impacts and possible ways to fix it. Familiar names, like President Reagan and Federal Reserve Chairman Alan Greenspan, surfaced repeatedly; repetitions tend to make such stories more memorable. Conversely, remembering was made more difficult because the stories were widely scattered. There were many months without coverage; months with multiple stories were rare.

The situation was similar for news about unemployment. ABC nightly news had nine stories, and CBS and NBC each had ten. NBC was the only network to cover more than one unemployment story in a single month. The good news for respondents asked about unemployment trends was that all of the networks publicized Department of Labor unemployment figures monthly during the second half of the year.

To sum up, irrespective of the use of a particular network, precise figures on unemployment and the deficit were available to citizens for situations covered routinely by government reports. Such reports are customarily distributed to news organizations, which usually publish them because the subject matter has broad impact and is something authentic that citizens should know. Besides, it is an inexpensive news item that has become a regular feature of an established news beat. Though it is unlikely that most people would pay close attention to such routine stories, it is important to note that the information was available. All too often, the news media are falsely blamed for public ignorance and criticized for slighting important facts, even when these facts were adequately reported.

The situation was more complex, and more typical, for information about environmental protection measures in the Reagan years. News stories did not match the NES survey questions, although there were multiple stories about particular environmental trouble spots.

ABC nightly news carried eleven stories about particular environmental policies for 1988, covering six distinct topics. NBC had nine stories, devoted to five different topics. CBS had seven stories on five topics. Acid rain and the greenhouse effect were discussed by all the networks, beach pollution in the Northeast was discussed in multiple stories by both CBS and NBC, and drinking-water pollution was covered by a single story on both ABC and NBC. Other topics, like air pollution or garbage removal, were covered by only one of the networks. ABC viewers were treated to the largest number of stories (11) and the richest political content, though none of the stories focused on overall appraisals of policy trends.

Newspaper Offerings

To take a closer look at the details that might have come to the public's attention in lengthier news offerings, we also analyzed newspaper coverage of the target topics, using the LexisNexis database. Like broadcasts, newspapers did cover hard data, such as budget deficit and unemployment figures, for which government reports were easily available.

The *New York Times* was an exceptionally ample source for budget deficit reports. The news in other papers was much sparser. The headlines of the 26 *New York Times* stories on the issue suggested that the deficit was a major problem and that various well-known, high-level political leaders were eager to reduce it. Three editorials about the problem further alerted readers to the fact that this was an important story. Similarly, 23 *New York Times* stories reported the trends in unemployment rates, giving specific comparative data. But, as is common, the periods selected for comparisons varied, and none of them matched the comparison span required by the 1988 NES survey questions. Readers would be able to learn about comparisons between the 1970s, when unemployment figures were exceptionally low, and 1988, but not about comparisons between 1980 and 1988.

As was true of broadcast stories about unemployment, there were multiple colorful examples through which aspects of environmental policies were brought to the attention of audiences. Again, the *New York Times* was most prolific, but other papers had multiple articles included in the large LexisNexis story pool. Most of these stories dealt with specific environmental problems in named locations, and what government and the private sector were doing about them. The range of specific stories covered in the newspapers differed from the stories aired by the networks. That is understandable, since newspapers tend to stress problems in their own localities, while networks take a broader, more national approach. Again, it would be very difficult to discern from reading these stories whether government attention to environmental protection was trending upward or downward. Some stories suggested more action; others suggested less.

As a final effort in evaluating the information supply, we randomly selected articles covering each of the target areas for closer scrutiny. True to journalists' penchant for being "neutral" by publishing clashing views on controversial issues, the stories were often more confusing than enlightening. For instance, how should a reader interpret a *New York Times* story that questioned the authenticity of the information that it cited? The *Times* quoted a study by the government's Office of Technology Assessment as concluding that "A lack of leadership and a poorly trained work force are weakening the Environmental Protection Agency's efforts to clean up the nation's hazardous waste sites." But then it cited respected sources who condemned the study, calling it "limited," "superficial," and based on "inadequate data" (Shabecoff, 1988).

News about progress on the environmental front was mostly mixed and qualified in various ways. For instance, one study of the evolution of environmental policies points out that "budget cuts and the weakening of environmental institutions took a serious toll in the l980s. Yet even the determined efforts of a popular president could not halt the long-term progress of environmental policy"

(Vig and Kraft, 1990: p. 15). That study also acknowledged the difficulty of making overall evaluations: "Environmental policies entail long-term commitments to broad social values and goals that are not easily quantified or measured. Short-term and highly visible costs are easier to measure than long-term, diffuse, and intangible benefits, and these differences often lead to intense debates over the value of environmental programs. Variable monitoring of environmental conditions and inconsistent collection of data over time also make it difficult to assess environmental trends" (Vig and Kraft, 1990: pp. 20–21).

As mentioned earlier, when stories presented comparative data, they used many different time periods for comparison, but most of them did not match the comparison periods required for answering the survey questions. When figures were given, they varied in the range of specifics that were covered, and they were often out of date. The most helpful story was a *New York Times* editorial (Anonymous, 1988) that reviewed the Reagan presidency on the eve of the 1988 Republican convention. It gave precise comparative figures on unemployment rates and the budget deficit. However, although it gave comparative data on several other policies, the environment was not mentioned.

The final score on the match between media coverage and survey questions about Reagan era policies is thus a mixed one. That raises questions about the accuracy and fairness of Professor Gilens's comments about the public's political ignorance. Attentive audiences could have learned necessary facts about the budget deficit and unemployment, especially if they watched nightly news television broadcasts and read the *New York Times,* which few do. But information about environmental policy trends was elusive, even in these media. Such a mixed outcome is likely to be fairly typical for most other policy issues about which Americans have been asked in surveys.

The 2000 Presidential Election Dispute

When voters are asked about unfolding events, looking at the match issues with a shorter focus yields somewhat more optimistic conclusions than the eight-year-long Reagan case. A very interesting example is media coverage of the disputed vote counts in the state of Florida during the 2000 presidential election and the many polls that measured the public's views about the unfolding events. The situation was very complex because of several technical challenges concerning the adequacy of vote-count procedures. The legality of decisions made by local authorities and courts was appealed to the Florida Supreme Court and the U.S. Supreme Court. The outcome of the presidential election hinged on these issues.

To check journalists' and pundits' comments about the Florida situation and compare them to the questions that pollsters asked at the time, we analyzed relevant stories in 15 newspapers using the LexisNexis database. Even though television is the most widely used source of political information, we picked print media because they are more likely to present the kinds of details that respondents need to know to answer poll questions correctly. The papers were the *Atlanta Journal-Constitution, Boston Globe, Chicago Sun-Times, Christian Science Monitor, Columbus Dispatch, Denver Post, Houston Chronicle, Los Angeles Times, Miami Herald, Minneapolis Star Tribune, New York Times, Omaha World Herald, Seattle Times, Times Picayune,* and *Washington Post.* We also checked the Web version of CNN.

There were major discrepancies between the content of the news stories and the poll questions. Out of the 31 issues raised in various polls, 13 had been nearly totally ignored by all the media, and another 10 were touched only lightly. That leaves just 8 that were covered extensively. Out of these, only 2 issues covered by poll questions were the key issues featured in news stories. Given these facts, it would be reasonable to expect a large percentage of incorrect or missing answers. Surprisingly, a majority of the respondents to the poll questions nonetheless gave reasonable answers when asked during the postelection weeks in 2000. The probable explanation is that they drew on relevant knowledge stored in memory.

For example, when asked whether the election outcome should be decided by the U.S. Supreme Court, Florida courts, or the U.S. Congress, majorities opted for the institution that Americans respect most, which is the U.S. Supreme Court. They also opted that, in line with what they remembered from previous presidential elections, the candidate winning the electoral college vote should be president. The fact that his opponent had more popular votes did not sway them, even though most indicated a preference for choosing a president solely on the basis of the popular vote.

Conclusion

As our two cases show, matching news reports with poll questions is a problem, but it is not as serious as it seems when we put it into a larger context. Many people have a warehouse of political information stored in their memories and draw on it when they try to make sense of current happenings.

Still, the matching problems that we have discussed raise fundamental questions about the types of queries that should be asked to test the adequacy of citizens' political knowledge and the adequacy of the news media as suppliers of information that monitorial citizens need. Our findings also raise questions about the fairness of judging the American public's civic intelligence based on responses to questions that only those with access to elite media can be expected to answer.

CHAPTER THREE
TELEVISION DRAMAS AS NEWS SOURCES

The previous chapters have presented evidence that people pay attention to ongoing political developments and form reasonably sound political opinions. Evidence also shows that a broad array of news platforms provides a plentiful news diet. But all is not well when we examine audience behavior.

In this chapter, we will look at some alternative sources of news and explain how we analyzed their stories about politics. We also sample what content they offer and what information viewers are likely to learn.

Defecting from Traditional News

Audience measurement data reveal a steady decline in the numbers of people who read newspapers and news magazines, watch television and cable news, or listen to news broadcasts. Figure 3.1 provides an illustration of this decline for the most popular news medium, television, over a 30-year period.

Using a mere ten-year measurement interval, we find steep drops in attention on most platforms. In 2009, only 71 percent of the public received most of its national and international news from television, compared to 82 percent in 1999. For newspapers, the 2009 percentage of readers was 33 percent, down from 42 percent

**Figure 3.1 Declines in Evening News Viewers,
November 1980 to November 2009**

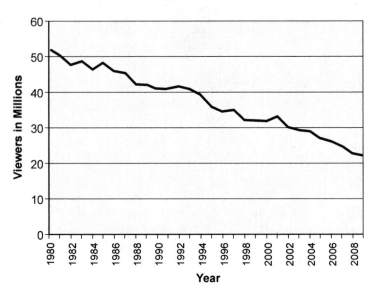

Source: "The State of the News Media," Pew Research Center, 2010, quoting Nielsen Media Research Center.

ten years earlier. Radio news listeners dropped from 49 percent in 1998 to 35 percent in 2008 (Pew Research Center, 2008c, 2009).

It is somewhat comforting that other Pew surveys show that many people who shunned traditional news sources professed to get their political information from shows labeled as entertainment. They mentioned satirical shows, like Comedy Central's *The Daily Show* with Jon Stewart, which 23 percent said they watched fairly often, and *The Colbert Report,* which 19 percent followed to some extent. They also mentioned hearing about politics on comedy offerings like the *Late Show* with David Letterman and *The Tonight Show* with Jay Leno. Thirty-three percent of the survey respondents claimed to watch these shows more or less regularly (Pew Research Center, 2008c).

The frequent mention of such shows, and the fact that 56 percent of respondents to the Pew survey also watch news magazine shows—such as *60 Minutes, 20/20,* and *Dateline*—indicates that "serious" news platforms are not the only sources from which average people receive political information. Candidates for political office have known this for quite some time.

Candidates acknowledge that entertainment shows are effective channels for dispensing political information by using them regularly for campaigning. Ross Perot (in 1992) and Fred Thompson (in 2008) even chose entertainment shows as the initial launching pad for their presidential campaign (Jones, 2005; Pew Research Center, 2008c). Other noteworthy presidential appearances on comedy shows include Richard Nixon on *Laugh-In,* Bill Clinton on *The Arsenio Hall Show,* and Barack Obama on *The Oprah Winfrey Show* and *The Daily Show* (in 2008). Obama's Republican opponent in 2008, John McCain, traveled the talk-show circuit with visits to *The Daily Show* and *The View,* among others.

Enjoying satire and comedy requires at least a moderate degree of familiarity with the subject matter that is the target of the satirical critique or joke. Therefore, it is no surprise that the audience for these satirical shows tends to be young, well educated, and interested in politics. When educational levels of audiences are compared, viewers of Jon Stewart's *The Daily Show* have been considerably above average in terms of academic achievements (Baumgartner and Morris, 2008, Chapters 14–16).

That raises the question of whether there are other entertainment news sources that are more suited to the tastes and skills of people who are less interested in political news or whose educational background makes it difficult for them to make sense of news stories, especially when the stories appear in print, rather than audio or audiovisual formats.

In this chapter, I will demonstrate and argue that many popular television dramas serve as alternative sources for understanding the political world. They tell engaging stories, and their story lines are embedded in situations that closely resemble current political environments.

Making Sense of Politics via Entertainment Venues

The main story lines of dramas rarely are concerned explicitly with politics, but the featured events play out in settings that reflect contemporary political conditions and dilemmas. Audience members watch these shows because they are interested in the story line. They do not focus on the settings, but they are definitely aware of them. How much, if anything, do the dramas teach them about politics? Hypotheses about the answer to that question vary widely. They include the following predictions:

- Political content will be ignored
- Political content will be noticed but discounted as fictional
- Political content will be noticed and taken seriously
- Political content will not be noticed but lead to passive learning anyhow.

My research findings support the hypothesis that learning from political dramas is mostly passive, which means that audiences absorb politically relevant information without an explicit intention to learn. In fact, when asked about what they have learned from watching the shows, they often deny that they have learned anything aside from the explicit story line. But I am getting ahead of my story.

In this chapter, I sketch out how my assistants and I designed and executed the research on learning about politics from entertainment shows. The inquiry began as a decade-long study of the content of popular television dramas. We wanted to explore what that entertainment genre might be able to contribute to the public's political information supply, given its story lines and dramatic formats. The research culminated in an interview-based study that analyzed what real-life audiences had actually learned from nine specific dramas. These dramas involved typical problematic public-policy areas like health care, organized crime, and the quality of government performance.

Our focus was on the broad policy realms that have engaged publics throughout history, rather than the specific details depicted in story episodes. Specifics of events are constantly changing, as are the ways in which stories about political happenings are transmitted. But the basic concerns embedded in the policy realms remain the same. People will always care about health-care issues, crime control, and the behavior of men and women charged with carrying out government functions.

Chapter Four presents a broad picture of the kinds of information that a sample of American viewers learned from watching diverse serial dramas that were popular when the interviews were conducted. Chapter Five enriches the story based on more detailed analysis of the interview transcripts. It tabulates what audience members told interviewers in response to various questions. In addition to the American responses, Chapter Five shows how the same questions were answered by a sample of Dutch and Greek viewers who had seen the same shows in their homelands. We wondered whether their responses would be comparable, or whether they would reflect the unique political cultures prevalent in the Netherlands, Greece, and the United States.

What Dramas Teach Viewers

The interview-based segments of our study about political learning had three major goals. Most important, we designed the interviews to ascertain whether regular adult watchers actually learned about politics from a particular television drama. Did exposure to the politically relevant settings that surrounded the story's characters teach viewers something—anything—about politics and, if so, what was it?

Answering these questions required assessing the contents of the shows about which we were interrogating audience members. We could not establish whether there was a link between people's political insights and the stories presented in the dramas without first exploring the content of these dramas.

Accordingly, our second research goal was to scrutinize the content of several genres of television dramas that were popular when this study began. Some of these dramas are no longer in production, although reruns are broadcast regularly and attract avid past fans as well as new viewers. But the themes around which the earlier productions revolved remain alive and vigorous. There are new crime shows, fresh examples of bumbling politicians, and updated versions of the challenges presented by serious diseases that afflict the human race.

The third goal actually emerged from conducting the research. Our audience research findings forced us to ponder the concept of *learning*. We had to consider what precisely it means to learn something about a political topic. What outcomes should we expect if viewers had learned something from the show, and how and what should we measure as evidence? Furthermore, it seemed important to track to what extent learning outcomes related to the concept of civic IQ, introduced in Chapter One. Pondering such questions led us to draw clear distinctions between *memorizing* and *understanding,* and to define and measure various levels of learning.

Television Drama Attractions

We thought that television serial dramas could be particularly promising sources for learning about politics for several reasons. These include their format and emotional effects, and their relevance to viewers' lives.

Storytelling Format

First of all, dramas tell stories, and most everyone loves stories. Aesop, the famous Greek teller of fables, already knew that circa 600 BC, and he was hardly the first one. Aesop's *The Wolf in Sheep's Clothing* teaches about deception and the need to be wary. *The Goose with the Golden Eggs* warns about greed and other excesses. If you want to teach people about ultimate consequences of their actions, success is most likely if the information is part of an engrossing story. In twenty-first century terms, that means that political problems can be made enticing by embedding them in popular television dramas. Story characters play their roles in graphic, visible, and audible settings that are currently relevant, making it easier for the audience to think that they are witnessing actual events unfolding before their eyes. It is easier to absorb information that is embedded in a recognizable context that resonates with other incoming information than to internalize information that is embedded in unfamiliar, often puzzling, contexts.

As mentioned earlier, many Americans distrust the news media. They find the typical political arguments pretentious and often unconvincing (Delli Carpini and Keeter, 1996). However, they are far more accepting when it comes to television dramas. Unlike most news stories, television dramas create suspense for their devoted audiences and keep their attention. After an episode has ended, many viewers continue to ponder the scenarios. They often discuss them with other viewers, and they are eagerly awaiting the next episode.

Emotion Effects

Dramatic events, especially when they are happening right before your eyes, tap into basic human feelings, like love and hate or sorrow and joy. That gives them emotional appeal, which is a tremendously important inducement for learning. People want to know what is happening, and they begin to care about the characters who are part of the story or who will be affected by the emotion-arousing events.

Emotional arousal is such a powerful stimulant of brain activity because it leads to release of hormones, like adrenaline, that sharpen perceptions and make them more memorable. Arousal makes it easier for people to process information and to commit it to memory.

Drama politics is also arousing because it brings political situations down to personal levels. Dramas "have challenged normative assumptions about who gets to speak about politics on television, what issues will be covered and in what manner, and how audiences can engage politics on television beyond simply deferring to expert knowledge" (Jones, 2005, p. *x*). Audience members feel empowered to make and express judgments about political situations. If the characters in the drama can do it, they can do it, too. They feel encouraged to form political impressions based on the happenings they witnessed when they watched these dramas.

Relevance Factors

Most of the stories told in popular television dramas deal with problems and dilemmas that are prominent in the lives of ordinary human beings at that time. That makes the story lines relevant to audiences who are facing similar problems themselves, see them in their environment, or can easily imagine that they might happen at some future time.

The political context in which the stories play out is subtle enough so that it does not repel viewers who dislike or even hate politics. In the long-running drama *Friends,* for instance, the characters deal with dating, marriage, divorce, and job responsibilities. Their experiences become realistic because they are cast in the context of issues then current in the news and widely discussed around the proverbial watercoolers or breakfast tables (Blythe, 2002; Jones, 1992). The flesh-and-blood characters in the drama personalize these contextual issues, demonstrating how they actually impact average people's lives.

Seeing live actors cope with the problems of the times repeatedly makes these lessons in contemporary affairs very meaningful. In fact, they are much more meaningful than the less personalized and less visualized stories used in straight public-affairs news programs.

During interviews or on bulletin boards devoted to these dramas, viewers often report that they found themselves in situations that were similar to what was happening to the characters in the show. In fact, the shows were so involving that some viewers reported screaming at their television set when bad things were happening to their favorite characters, or even dreaming about characters in the show. Their dream scenarios did not necessarily replicate happenings on the show. In fact, viewers' imaginations often created totally new spin-off situations.

Tying stories to characters that have become familiar and real makes it easier for audience members to remember the events that are happening in the dramas. If audience members are engrossed in the story, their brains actually register it like a personal experience. This is why most people are able to retain a large array of names and faces of entertainment personalities, along with facts about the roles that these people play in the dramas (Jones, 2005). By contrast, they have trouble remembering the names of political leaders. It is also easier to retain political information when it is told from the value-oriented perspectives that ordinary people use, rather than the issue-oriented perspectives of political elites (Thelen, 1996; Lembo, 2000; Delli Carpini and Williams, 2001; Jones, 2005).

Compared to the ease of grasping serial-drama politics, people often find it difficult to process political information presented by media platforms in typical news formats. Regular news stories commonly employ more stilted prose that ranks above the eighth-grade level in reading ease. Average citizens find it difficult to read. Regular news often features a series of contradictory facts and appraisals—X says it's right; Y says it's wrong—that viewers find confusing.

The politically relevant episodes in television dramas employ ordinary language and the kinds of discussion formats that people use over the backyard fence or at the bowling alley. Unlike regular news, the political dialogue in television dramas is "refreshingly honest, impassioned, diverse, stimulating, witty, and smartly commonsensical" (Jones, 2005, p. *ix*).

Story Length and Repetitions

The presentation format used for television serial dramas is also more conducive to learning than regular news offerings because the shows are much longer, ranging from 30 to 60 minutes. That compares to a running time of 1 to 3 minutes for the typical television news story. The longer time space means that television dramas can present a great deal more visual and aural information about story topics, including important contextual facts, than is possible in televised broadcasts and print news stories.

More information, particularly when it is pictorial rather than purely verbal, generally means more realistic insights and a greater array of memories available for recall. Telling stories through pictures also allows people with limited skills in the verbal language used in dramas to follow the story themes, even when they cannot understand many of the words.

Regularity of exposure to information is also a crucial factor. For fans of these shows, attendance is usually steady for the entire season. Many families set aside certain nights for watching favorite shows. The entire family—from the youngest to the oldest member—may watch together, making it a treasured group experience.

While attention to newspapers and news broadcasts tends to be sporadic, the vast majority of drama fans watch their favorites without fail. If they miss a particular episode, they often record the show, and then watch it at a convenient time once or more. There is much repetition of themes within and between shows. The episodes occur over a time span of 20 to 25 weeks, with new episodes added year after year. The originals are presented in reruns after that, drawing in millions of new viewers as well as old-timers. In fact, audience records for *The Sopranos* crime show indicate that many viewers saw each episode at least twice because it was packed with intriguing information.

Unlike newscasts that touch lightly on numerous happenings, television dramas tend to dwell on a limited number of major themes, which are linked through the involvement of the same familiar characters. The audience is exposed to this continuing story for multiple years in a row—more than 20 years in the case of *The Simpsons.* Repeated presentations of the same story deepen memory tracks.

Audience Sizes

The attractiveness of these serial dramas is confirmed by the huge audiences that they attract. We checked audience figures for five television shows that were very popular at the start of the twenty-first century: *The West Wing,* which deals with the U.S. presidency; the cartoon show *The Simpsons,* which satirizes small-town politics in the United States; the crime show *The Sopranos;*

ER (Emergency Room), which deals with important health-policy issues; and *Friends,* which pictures typical life situations that young Americans face.

We found that each of these five shows routinely attracted audiences ranging in size from 13 million to 23 million, compared to audiences of 6 to 8 million viewers for contemporary nightly network news shows.

For example *Friends,* captured an average U.S. audience of 23 million viewers per episode during its initial ten-year run. The numbers ranged from a low of 19.8 million to a high of 28 million (Johnson, 2004; Jones, 2005; Franklin, 2006).

The 2006 season finale of *CSI* attracted 25.4 million U.S. viewers. These figures omit the worldwide audience, which exceeds U.S. numbers.

In the 2006 *American Idol* contest, 63.4 million viewers voted in the election that determined the winner. That compares to 62 million who voted for President Bush in the 2004 presidential election (FootnoteTV, 2006).

The opening show of *The Sopranos* fourth season, despite its location on pay-cable HBO, surpassed all cable television audience ratings, including competing free shows (Potts, 2003).

Dramas as Real-World Behavior Models

The "CSI effect" is a recent example that demonstrates that many people learn from fictional television dramas like *CSI* (Crime Scene Investigation). Judges in criminal cases are complaining that jurors who have been ardent watchers of crime shows like *CSI* expect crime-fighting officials to employ the same sophisticated methods used in these shows to solve criminal cases. If the actual procedures in a real-life crime situation fall short of these fictional models, juries fail to convict, even when the evidence is strong by normal standards. Unfortunately, cramming crime stories into 60-minute shows tends to exaggerate the effectiveness of the methods, so that juries base their judgments on unrealistically high expectations (*The Economist,* April 22, 2010).

Similar effects have been observed in other areas of life. When people lack experience with the real situations, they draw on their vicarious experiences, which often come from television shows. In fact, information obtained from entertainment shows trumps information conveyed by news programs when the respective messages conflict (Delli Carpini and Williams, 2001; Baum, 2005).

A study of the views of life in America that Middle Eastern youths hold revealed that they trusted the images shown in popular American television dramas more than the images presented in nonfictional news stories (Graber, 2009). Other studies have investigated whether television dramas prime people's evaluations. In the case of *The West Wing*, there is solid evidence that the show primes viewers' thinking about real presidents (Holbert et al., 2003; Gans-Boriskin and Tisinger, 2005).

A series of studies of advertising messages embedded in entertainment shows also demonstrates learning (Bhatnagar et al., 2004; Green et al., 2004). When questioned about the advertisements, viewers rarely recall the precise words and pictures, but they often remember the gist of the message. Alternatively, they may not recall the message at all, but nonetheless apply the information that it contained in subsequent judgments that investigators ask them to make. This indicates they have internalized the message, even though they have forgotten the details of the stimulus.

Finally, there is evidence that various public-health messages conveyed in episodes of television dramas have a strong impact on many viewers. For example, the Center for Disease Control (CDC) worked with the producers of the popular daytime soap opera *The Bold and the Beautiful* to produce a subplot about HIV. The episode included the CDC's national sexually transmitted disease and AIDS hotline toll-free phone number. After the episode aired, the hotline was overwhelmed with calls from viewers. Callers wanted information about protection and testing, in line with the recommendations that were made by the show's protagonists (Kennedy et al., 2004). Many of the callers told interviewers that they had first learned about the hotline from the soap-opera episode. More than half claimed that the episode had inspired them to make lifestyle changes to protect their health.

The Master Research Design

Our research required two distinct approaches. We needed a content-analysis design that would capture the political information made available in drama episodes and an interview procedure that would detect what audiences had actually learned from this information. The following sections describe how we proceeded, along with the reasons that influenced the choice of the final design.

Lessons from the Shows

Our search for political information in television dramas moved from a wide-angle shot of the search territory to a narrow view of points of special interest. Like detectives in search of evidence, we explored all possible leads.

Analyzing Content

How did we analyze the content of the television dramas that our viewers saw? As mentioned, the development of political drama content analysis took place over several years. Initially, we analyzed the content of popular dramas just to establish whether they contained serious and substantial political information, and to record the subjects that were covered. We also checked to what degree the political facts depicted in the drama seemed accurate and informative compared to their real-world counterparts.

During later stages of the project, the analysis became more detailed and formal. When content analysis involved print news sources or message boards, we used standard content-analysis methods, including computer search functions, wherever available. Unfortunately, many message boards have no regular search capabilities, forcing us to read thousands of entries in search of the target information.

To verify the accuracy of coding, 10 percent of the content was checked by more than one coder, and their coding judgments were compared. Overall, agreement scores were in the 80 percent range or better (Lombard, 2010). From the start, our analyses showed that the television dramas that we had chosen for analysis, taken as a whole, featured ample politically relevant content. We also found that the information about political happenings was amazingly accurate, even in shows like *The West Wing*, which features a multitude of details about presidential activities in the White House.

From the general analysis of the broad thrust of the show, we progressed to analyzing the content of specific shows, again focusing on the topics that were discussed, the completeness and accuracy of the information, and the frames that were used. We paid particular attention to the emotion-arousing potential of these stories, including the presence or absence of cultural norm violations, which constitute exceptionally potent memory stimuli.

Coders were instructed to first provide a running account of what was happening in each episode. Next, they identified the main political information that the episode contained. They were instructed to avoid being introspective, because we wanted to focus on political information that would be obvious to most audience members. Just as is done in gestalt coding, coders began by using the words, sounds, and pictures of the story and its settings to determine the main idea—the *gestalt*—that an episode was intended to convey. The gestalt is fairly easy to identify because producers of television dramas tell their stories using common discourse to make sure that heterogeneous audiences can readily comprehend the intended meanings (Graber, 2001).

A caveat is in order. We know that audience members do not necessarily extract the intended meanings from a show's messages. In fact, they often endow the messages with their own unique meanings, especially if they are looking for specific information, rather than merely following wherever the story may lead (Silverblatt, 1995; Swanson et al., 1998; Blythe, 2002; Kozlowski, 2005). However, while idiosyncratic interpretations are common, they do not preclude simultaneous attention to the intended meaning of story messages. The majority of the audience tends to stick with these intended message meanings, which they interpret in light of shared cultural and societal experiences (Graber, 2001).

The Range of Information

Table 3.1 presents the topics covered by the information reported in a total of 91 episodes featured in just five popular television dramas during one television season. The sample includes the following:

- 22 episodes offered in *The West Wing*'s second season
- 22 episodes in the fifth season of *The Simpsons*
- 13 episodes that made up the fourth season of *The Sopranos*
- 27 episodes from *ER* in that show's second season
- 7 *Friends* episodes featured in its second season

The table is divided into ten information categories.

I would expect agreement that most of the subject areas listed in Table 3.1 constitute valuable political information that enhances citizens' political IQ. I would not expect agreement about which of these subject areas are truly valuable for the civic IQ and which should be deemed trifling. Suffice it to say that the composite list represents incontrovertible evidence that these shows are rich sources of significant political information, albeit not necessarily focused on topics like electoral politics or Beltway antics, which are staples in regular news.

Does Drama Content Matter?

Yes, drama content matters. The stories told by the dramas were scrutinized much more carefully by various observers than we had imagined, largely because real-world consequences were anticipated. For instance, some websites, such as footnote.com (http://newsaic.com), specialize in analyzing questions raised by political issues aired in television dramas. These websites provide comments about the accuracy, incidence, and applicable laws for the situations in question. Devotees of these sites were likely to go

Table 3.1 What Citizens Can Learn from Entertainment Shows

Category	Examples
How the Federal Government Works	Dynamics between the president, his staff, Congress, foreign leaders
	Interplay of multiple unrelated policy concerns
	Steps in turning bills into laws
	How pocket vetoes work
	Dominance of federal laws over state laws
	Constitutional limits on congressional power
	Functions performed by the FDA and the Coast Guard
General Political Issues and Public Attitudes	How public opinion works
	How lobbies operate
	Antigay sentiments in Congress and among U.S. population
	Struggles over framing issues effectively in a politically correct manner
	Wisdom of legalizing gambling to solve a community's financial problems
	Wisdom of offering tax incentives to influence economic decisions
How Politicians Misbehave	How police act stupidly and engage in immature misbehavior
	How public officials excuse their failures
	How public agencies give preferred treatment to influential people
	How inspectors in regulated industries accept bribes
Citizen Rights and Services	First and Fourteenth Amendment rights of American citizens
	Defendants in lawsuits are innocent until proven guilty
	Free legal services for the poor
	Medical service rights of uninsured patients
	Suicide prevention hotlines
	Witness relocation programs
	How public libraries function

Table 3.1 (continued)

Category	Examples
How Various Laws Work	Consumer safety laws
	Medical malpractice laws
	Immigration laws
	Laws about drug dealing, possession, use
	Laws and rules about gambling
	Laws about granting parole
	Homeowners' rights of self-defense during home invasion
	Landlords' obligation to fix natural disaster damage
	Money deposits create contractual obligations
Explaining Law Violations	Smuggling of contraband is profitable because gains exceed fines
	People manipulate tax incentives for private gain
	People hide money overseas to shield it from taxation
	Mobsters buy real estate through shell companies to defraud HUD
	Police and the FBI keep mob activities under constant surveillance
	Crooked police cooperate with mobsters to protect gambling
	Mobsters use prison phones to conduct business
	Mob mentality causes normal people to act irrationally
Family Law	How couples complete pre-marriage formalities
	Child custody and adoption rules
	Joint custody of children after divorce
	Creating trusts for children
	Notifying parents about teen pregnancies
	Legal rights of abuse victims: children, spouses, elders
	Pre-surgery consent requirements
	"Do not resuscitate" rules

Table 3.1 (continued)

Category	Examples
Lifestyles	Appropriateness of behavior and discussions regarding sex, drugs, gambling
	Appropriateness of gender roles, age-related activities, attire, language
	Appropriateness of value structure: obsession with youth, sports heroes
	How connections and good looks trump work skills
	How children learn to relish TV cruelty and imitate it
	Urban gangs are violent
	How people earn PhDs and Nobel Prizes
	How Jews celebrate Hanukkah
	Rules of conduct enforced within the Mafia hierarchy
Health-Care Issues	Abortion and infertility
	Viagra and heart failure
	Asbestos and health damage
	Prevention issues: gun accidents
	AIDS, prevention and treatment
	Child/spouse/elder abuse
	Problems caused by uninsured patients
	Hospital overcrowding
	Problems caused in health-care facilities by language diversity
	Drug addicts who fake injuries to get drugs
	Patient privacy protection
	Paramedics' functions
	Need for defensive medical procedures
American and European History	History of right to vote in the U.S.
	History of slavery in the U.S.
	History of Columbus and Columbus Day
	Facts about politics of Hitler, Nixon, Clinton

public when they detected serious errors, and they expected that their complaints would be echoed in the news media.

Further confirmation that many Americans think that the content of television serial dramas is quite influential comes from news stories and editorials that express concerns about the real-world impact of dramas. The attitudes of television characters like Jack Bauer from the show *24* are a good example. Bauer is a key member of a fictional Counter Terrorist Unit (CTU) based in Los Angeles. His main job is prevention of major terrorist attacks on the United States.

Bauer's frequent use of torture to gather information has been widely debated. The program routinely includes scenes of physical and psychological torture. Perhaps most controversial were a number of characters whose exclusive job it was to torture captured enemies to extract "ticking-bomb" information. The torturers succeed in saving the country from major disasters, like a bomb or other device that has been planted to destroy a major airport or government building. Torture was essential to induce the captured enemies to confess the information needed to forestall the disaster.

The New Yorker magazine reported in February 2007 that the dean of the U.S. Military Academy at West Point, accompanied by military and FBI interrogators, met with the producers of *24* to complain that the show exaggerated the effectiveness of torture as an interrogation technique. The interrogators expressed concern that episodes in the drama might encourage soldiers to see torture as a useful and justified, and even patriotic tactic in the War on Terror (Mayer, 2007). *The New Yorker* story opposed the *24* story line, and its criticism was echoed by other commentators, who argued that repeated use of the ticking time-bomb scenario could sanitize torture in the public consciousness.

Public debates about the political impact of the show on soldiers, the general public, and publics around the world included high-level civilian government officials like Michael Chertoff, then Secretary of Homeland Security, and Supreme Court Justice Clarence Thomas.

Lessons from the Viewers

We began our research about the impact of the dramas on the audience's civic IQ with several traditional experiments. They were conducted with political science students at a large Midwestern urban university. Field tests with a sample of actual adult viewers of the dramas followed.

Laboratory Experiments

We chose the experiment approach because it is easiest to identify the relationship between stimuli and their impact in a controlled laboratory environment, where distracting stimuli can be kept to a minimum. For example, if you want to know whether the sound of a police siren leads to sharp spikes in people's pulse rates, you should not take pulse readings in a location where there are already many potentially frightening sounds and sights. In a laboratory environment, the siren sounds would likely be the sole alarming stimulus.

Before actually testing how much the students had learned from watching selected episodes of *The Sopranos*, we administered a survey to detect if any of the students were political sophisticates. Sophisticates' learning patterns were apt to differ from patterns seen in more politically naïve individuals. The survey included three "political sophistication" questions borrowed from studies of learning from soft news (Baum, 2003, 2005), two questions about the kinds of political issues that *The Sopranos* show features, and eight questions designed to assess each student's media-consumption habits.

We hypothesized that respondents who predominantly watch hard news would respond more accurately to the political sophistication measures. Respondents who mostly watched soft news would pay closer attention to events in fictional television dramas, including the political aspects covered in *The Sopranos*. These expectations were confirmed, and have become one of many examples of how message meanings can vary drastically depending on the intellectual baggage that audience members bring to the table (Chong and Druckman, 2010).

Following the pretest survey, respondents saw a half hour of clips from *The Sopranos* (season 4, episodes 3 and 7). These clips focused on housing and urban development issues that involved the U.S. Department of Housing and Urban Development (HUD). They also raised the touchy question about whether Christopher Columbus should be considered an American hero or a villain who abused indigenous populations. We thought that the students would be unfamiliar with these two political issues, especially with the abuse accusations leveled against Christopher Columbus.

After one week's postexposure delay to allow normal forgetting to set in, we asked the respondents to complete a second survey. That survey consisted of seven questions regarding political aspects covered in *The Sopranos* and two questions that requested the respondents to list all sources they had used to answer the political aspect questions. Roughly half of the students said that they had learned about either HUD or Columbus, and listed *The Sopranos* episode as a source of their information. We credited the students with "learning" if they had no idea about what HUD was or listed no negative attributes about Christopher Columbus in the pretest, but knew what HUD was and how it worked or listed negative attributes about Christopher Columbus in the posttest.

Our open-ended question format gave us insights about the reasoning processes that led respondents to their answers. Their word choices and framing of the arguments provided us with important cues, as did comparisons of the pretests and posttests. We particularly watched for major changes in reasoning. We suspected that watching the show had been a learning experience whenever survey participants responded with the identical or similar terminology, language, and descriptions that had been used in *The Sopranos* episode. For instance, respondents might describe the HUD process as "minorities get housing by taking over inexpensive houses and then rebuilding them using the organization's funds." That was the precise wording that had been used in the show.

In the second week of the experiment, we also conducted focus groups in which we asked the students several questions about the political aspects covered in *The Sopranos*. Many of the students' responses demonstrated that they had learned, or at least could repeat, assertions that were covered in *The Sopranos*. For example, nearly all the participants claimed taxpayers would foot the bill for HUD scams—an assumption specifically mentioned in the clips.

Moreover, the evidence suggests that the participants were influenced by the class and race bias pictured in the clips. They claimed that well over 90 percent of those receiving HUD benefits are African-American. That is a large overestimation. Additionally, when the respondents were asked to give examples of how one could "scam the federal government," many alluded to a scam depicted in *The Sopranos* as a very realistic scenario and said that it occurs often in real life. This supports the claim that their responses were influenced by the episode.

Of course, we cannot prove decisively that participants learned what they did from *The Sopranos* and only *The Sopranos*. Information environments are complex; countless external factors could have influenced the participants' responses. For example, exposure to the show could have prompted them to use search engines to learn more about HUD and Christopher Columbus. The strength of our claim is also undermined by the absence of control groups, such as non-*Sopranos* viewers. Contrary to our initial intentions, financial constraints kept us from examining whether respondents who had not seen the shows gave substantially different answers than actual *Sopranos* viewers.

Nonetheless, the evidence of learning from *The Sopranos* clips during the experimental study is strong. Not only did half of the respondents mention the show as a source of their information for answering the questions, but half of the total sample also used similar language, terminology, and examples as portrayed in the clips. The likelihood of that happening without seeing the show is slim.

Field Tests

After these traditional experiments—student samples, laboratory settings, pretests, stimulus administrations, and posttests—yielded promising results, we proceeded to field studies of adult populations. All along, we had planned to take this important step if the experiments showed that television dramas could, indeed, teach viewers important things about politics.

There were many reasons for testing our laboratory results in the real world. Personally, I have always been uneasy about using students as subjects in experiments designed to test attitudes of the general adult population. Students are a unique breed. Most are very young adults still in their formative stages when it comes to developing political opinions. They lack the experiences that come from living in society and observing the unfolding political world under a variety of different conditions and over extended periods of time. Student populations also are more highly motivated to learn and more skilled in learning than the average adult who finished formal schooling decades earlier.

Furthermore, experimental environments suffer from being sterile and unnatural. Recent studies have shown that when laboratory effects are compared to the effects of similar stimuli in field situations, the effects in the laboratory tend to be stronger and sometimes in the opposite direction (Barabas and Jerit, 2010). We wanted to test learning by adults in more natural settings and under more natural conditions.

An additional incentive for doing field studies was the fact that they would allow us to try out some unconventional research approaches. We were eager to avoid the usual interview settings, where investigators, rather than viewers, choose the examples of political content that become the focus of follow-up questions. We hoped that our subjects would draw on political content of their own choice, as free as possible from the investigator's dominance. We also wanted our interviews to take place in a familiar environment: the viewers' own homes.

We avoided the widely used pretest phases because they run the risk of sensitizing respondents and altering their normal behaviors because they are reacting to their perceptions of the nature of the research. Besides, pretests of respondents' knowledge about a broad subject area are always inadequate, because they can explore only a small slice of the information that respondents bring to the situation. Short of deep psychological analyses of each research participant, ordinary pretests cannot detail the full range of each subject's psychological traits and experiences that come into play in reaction to a particular stimulus.

Our concerns about potentially harmful effects of pretests suggested that it would be advisable to use a cold-call approach. That meant that we would call a prospective interview subject's telephone number and solicit an immediate interview with the person who had been identified as a regular watcher of a specific drama. The cold-call approach worked most of the time. Nearly all interviews were completed during the initial call, although a few did require rescheduling to honor the respondent's time schedule. Telephone interviews averaged 20 minutes in length. We recorded them with the respondent's permission.

Sample Selection

The main problem we faced in constructing our viewer sample was identification of individuals who were regular viewers of specific popular shows. We solved that problem by developing a broad base of "informants" who would provide us with names and telephone numbers of potential subjects who were regular watchers of the specified dramas and were likely to consent to our request for an immediate interview.

The informant base started with a sizable group of students from the university where the original experiments had been done. We requested their help because the university has a very ethnically and economically diverse student population. We asked the students to give us contact information for family members and friends who were regular watchers of our television dramas and who, in their opinion, would be willing to be interviewed about these shows. In addition, personal friends and family members gave us similar leads.

To broaden the informant base, we also asked for help from randomly chosen members of chat rooms, people who gather at taverns that play the shows on designated nights, senior citizens living in group homes with television rooms, and authors of message board postings. Luckily, we were able to accumulate a lengthy list of names and telephone numbers and to reach most of these avid viewers. Nearly all agreed to be interviewed.

Question Selection

We began with the traditional idea that we would focus the research on learning patterns that might differ depending on the viewer's demographic and political characteristics and interests. The focus would be on the information the viewer had learned from the political content depicted in recent episodes of nine shows that we had content-analyzed.

Our array of shows for this phase of the research included *ER, The West Wing, Lost, 24, Family Guy, The Simpsons, The Sopranos, Grey's Anatomy,* and *CSI.* Content analysis had confirmed that these dramas regularly featured situations that related to contemporary political situations. We also knew that they drew huge audiences, so that their impact on political learning in the United States might be substantial.

The West Wing and *24* were the most overtly political shows in the group. They deal with activities involving a government modeled on the U.S. national government. *ER* and *Grey's Anatomy* involve health-policy issues. *Grey's Anatomy* even sponsors a website that discusses the medical conditions involved in the episodes. *The Sopranos* and *CSI* deal with issues of crime. *Lost* deals with issues of science, cultural diversity, and the problems of an anarchic society. *The Simpsons* and *Family Guy* are cartoon shows that satirize real-life situations and often rely on political content for their comedy. In the case of *The Simpsons,* that involves multiple political issues that confront public officials and citizens in small-town America.

The interviews began with open-ended questions that simply asked people what they had learned from their favorite shows, and then probed for details about whatever they had said. The open format allowed participants to choose the areas of knowledge that they linked to the show. Interviewer-chosen, closed-ended questions could easily fail to capture much of what respondents had actually learned. Asking every respondent the same questions would therefore waste valuable interview time on nonexistent or marginally relevant memories.[1]

To get responses to specific aspects of political learning, we followed up with more targeted questions about particular politically relevant incidents that the respondent had not mentioned previously. We also tested whether respondents could apply the information to a hypothetical situation that we posed on the assumption that ability to use information connotes genuine understanding beyond memorization. For example, if characters in the show obtained a deferment for jury duty by phoning a jury helpline, we might concoct a similar scenario and ask respondents how they would go about postponing jury duty and about the excuses most likely to win a deferment.

In the course of interviewing, it became clear that the varied backgrounds and experiences that people brought to the television story were key factors in determining how they targeted their attention and how they used the information. For instance, two nurses who watched *ER* paid little attention to issues that related to the nature of medical care in U.S. public hospitals because that information was familiar and therefore dispensable, except when it ran counter to their experiences. By contrast, people outside the health professions related to issues such as the differential treatment of people with and without insurance and the problems that arise when there are bed shortages, operating-room shortages, and shortages of blood needed for transfusions.

Lessons from the Interviews

When we analyzed the transcripts of the interviews, we rediscovered that simple answers to seemingly simple questions tend to be volatile. Answers change when questions are worded differently or asked in a different context. That is why we used multiple primes to tap into diverse niches of memory.

Second-thought revisions of answers are common in response to ideas that are spurred by the interview questions. For example, most of our participants told us, in direct response to a question early in the interview, that the shows had never taught them anything that they could use in their own lives. Nonetheless, during the course of the interview, everyone told us numerous things that she or he had learned and used or planned to use in the future. Some of them even reconsidered their initial answers and told us that they had not realized, when first asked about it, how much the shows had taught them about a variety of issues. It obviously takes multiple primes to tap into dormant or underdeveloped niches of memory, without altering memories in the process.

We also rediscovered that the interactions between television shows and viewers are akin to a conversation in which the ideas from the show and the ideas the viewer brings to the show become thoroughly intermingled (Delli Carpini and Williams, 2001). It is impossible to unscramble the components that have gone into each respondent's answers. When people are knowledgeable about matters discussed in the show, neither they nor we can tell with precision which aspects of their knowledge were formulated during the show or acquired before or afterward.

Conclusion

The television dramas that were the stimulus material for our interviews stimulated a broad array of diverse answers. This pool of individual responses constitutes a rich sample of actual reactions to information supplied by the television serial dramas.

The pooled reactions provide insights about the types of learning that take place akin to insights produced by Q methodology, which assesses the factors that influence people when they choose among available perspectives (Brown, 2008). It involves collecting a broad array of observations and reactions about a specific subject area and asking individuals to rank-order these comments. For example, disparate comments about a proposed health-care plan might be rank-ordered in terms of how well they matched the ranker's priorities, cost considerations, or the availability of appropriate health-care facilities. Similarly, our respondents sampled their memories when they answered our interview questions. They shared some of their stored perspectives, but not all of them.

What specific insights and facts did our interview participants learn from the political information embedded in the shows that they watched regularly? Did they become smarter about their rights as citizens or health-care issues, or even American and European history, based on the television drama episodes that they watched so intently? This chapter has set the scene for exploring that inquiry. It has dissected the unique characteristics of the television drama genre, and it has laid out the general research design for our investigation. The next two chapters focus on actual learning from dramas, first in broad outlines (Chapter Four) and then in detail (Chapter Five).

CHAPTER FOUR
INSIGHTS ABOUT TELEVISION DRAMAS

WHAT AMERICANS TOLD US

What did we find when we actually interviewed American viewers about the sorts of things they had learned from their favorite television dramas? This chapter begins with an overview of the terrain that lays out the topics covered in the television dramas that our interviewees had been watching. Comments about their overall reactions to these shows follow. To enlarge the pool of audience reactions to serial drama fare, we will also look at the thrust of the comments that viewers posted on websites associated with our shows.

Systematic, detailed analysis of the actual interview transcripts takes place in Chapter Five. That chapter also presents the results of interviews conducted in the Netherlands and Greece. The European interviews cover samples of viewers selected in the same manner as their American counterparts, who were exposed to the same dramas on their native Dutch or Greek television. The reactions of the European viewers allow us to assess the impact of cultural differences on political learning.

Political Tales: What the Viewers Saw

In preparation for interviewing the drama fans, we scrutinized nine prime-time television dramas for political content likely to interest average folks. Here are our choice rationales:

- For those who might genuinely care about politics at the top levels of government, we included *The West Wing* and *24* because of their overtly political content about American national and international politics.
- For folks who were more focused on the grassroots level of politics, we selected the long-lived *Simpsons* cartoon show, which features local-level politics stories.
- We chose *ER* and *Grey's Anatomy* because these shows deal with perennially vital issues of health policy.
- *CSI* and *The Sopranos* represent the ever-popular crime show genre.
- *Lost* presents a mixture of issues ranging from science to cultural diversity to problems of an anarchic society.
- We picked *Family Guy* as a cartoon show that satirizes real-life situations and occasionally relies on political content for its comedy.[1]

We found that the shows differed greatly in the richness of their political content. *The West Wing* ranked highest, with every episode illuminating aspects of presidential politics. In fact, the producers of *The West Wing* had been hired in part because they were fully familiar with actual presidential politics. Their expertise allowed them to make each episode as authentic as possible (Beavers, 2002; Gans-Boriskin and Tisinger, 2005).

Nonetheless, whenever particular subject matters are chosen for inclusion in drama episodes or in regular news stories, that choice creates the distorted view that these situations are paramount. For instance, *The West Wing* frequently dwells on communication and image problems in the White House, and what might happen if they were mishandled. That exaggerates the importance of image issues in presidential decisions. In real life, image issues are very important, but not necessarily the deciding factors in decision-making.

Three other shows—*24, The Sopranos,* and *The Simpsons*—also rank highly in richness of political content. Nearly every episode contains some sort of political information.

The Sopranos features the highest number of incidents that violate cultural norms, making the show especially arousing and memorable. The characters constantly use foul language and act in ways that epitomize the stereotype of Italians as Mafiosos engaged in criminal ventures. The images are so graphic and seem so authentic that they have angered many people, including those who do not ordinarily watch the show but hear about it.

The Sopranos has sparked major public protests, and there have been threats of lawsuits and attempts to pass laws to prohibit the show from linking gangsters to Italian roots (Lavery, 2002; Fields, 2004). These strong reactions show how seriously people take the fictional events that transpire in entertainment shows, especially when evildoers belong to demographic minority groups.

The Simpsons also deals with social norm violations, such as making fun of various religions, but it does so much more subtly than *The Sopranos,* and in a more satirical mode (Scanlan and Feinberg, 2000). In fact, viewers who are unaware of *The Simpsons'* tongue-in-cheek approach could easily miss the satire and take the gist of the episodes at face value.

Next in line in terms of providing a wealth of politically relevant information are *ER, Grey's Anatomy,* and *CSI*. Political messages are more intermittent in these shows. They are scarce in *Lost* and *Family Guy.* From those shows, audiences learn more about day-to-day living than about political concerns.

In sum, what audiences can learn from television dramas—or any other information source—varies dramatically in quality, quantity, and subject matter. Opportunities for learning about political issues, for example, are far more plentiful for viewers of *The Sopranos* than for aficionados of *Lost*. Similar differences hold true, of course, for nonfiction newscasts.

Just as specifics of the political information differ, so does the resonance of these political issues with each viewer's fund of prior information. What each viewer learns from each show depends on information stored in individual memories and on the viewer's long-standing or short-range interests at the time. People learn selectively.

This chapter presents details from four of the nine shows as examples of the kind of political information that our interviewees actually received. The tables that list the information are divided into four information categories that represent different types of lessons for viewers: Process Information, Facts, Context Information, and Insights. The significance of recognizing the diverse roles that these categories play in learning about politics is discussed in much greater detail in Chapter Six. Here, it suffices to simply identify them.

Viewers encounter *process information* when dramas enact specific events realistically on the screen, so that viewers become eyewitnesses who experience the information vicariously. *Facts* refers to mentioning explicit facts. Examples are proper names, dates, rules, and detailed statements about policy positions. *Context information* refers to the settings in which dramas and other events are embedded, like a busy medical practice or a tropical island. Settings may suggest particular local conditions and social and political climates, while *insights* refers to particular bits of potentially useful information that is peripheral to the plot. For example, the tips may be about a free public service or the location of a project that is hiring workers.

Politics in The West Wing

Overall, *The West Wing* provides excellent insights into the kinds of issues that occupy an American president's time and about the role played by the president's Chief of Staff and his assistant, and the large team of people involved in White House business. It becomes clear that the president relies heavily on his inner circle for advice and support. The importance of presidential aides is highlighted by showing them repeatedly on screen, even when the president is absent (Beavers, 2002).

Sequential episodes illustrate the enormity of the president's job over and over again. Obviously, President Bartlet must cope simultaneously with huge controversial domestic and foreign-policy issues, such as the nation's education policies, the high price of prescription medicines, AIDS epidemics in Africa, and rocky U.S. relations with China. He gets little help from the opposition party. The disdain for conservative Republican politics is palpable in the president's and his team's body language and various asides throughout.

The show also makes it clear that, in addition to developing policies, the president has arduous, time-consuming administrative duties, like making appointments to high government positions, speaking to politically important interest groups, and meeting with foreign leaders. All in all, *The West Wing* presidency looks like an overwhelming job, even when many capable assistants are on hand.

Several episodes focus on the strained relations between the president and Republicans (as well as Democrats) in Congress, along with strategies to soothe ruffled feelings. There is even a silver lining to the problems caused by conflict. President Bartlet explains that the waning power of a lame-duck Congress gives him an exceptional opportunity to look like a strong leader who wins his battles. Viewers are made aware of the weak party loyalty among both Democrats and Republicans and how that makes it possible to persuade members of either party to defect from their party's stands. Such intricate relationships are difficult to convey in words, but they become crystal clear when observed in action.

The vistas of government at the highest levels disseminated by *The West Wing* are generally very positive. President Bartlet, who is a Clintonesque Democrat, and his staff are dedicated to working for the public good. There is no hint of corruption. In fact, the images are so good that cynical viewers may dismiss what they see as sugar-coated reality. Others may still believe that politics is dirty business, yet sense that presidents mean well and that the government functions reasonably efficiently overall.

Table 4.1 presents examples of the type of information found in *The West Wing*.

The information that is so richly abundant in *The West Wing* falls into the process information category because it gives viewers vicarious experiences. By reenacting relevant situations, process

Table 4.1 *The West Wing* **Information Samples**

Information Types	Examples
Process	Interactions between president and Congress; interactions between president and staff members; interplay of policy concerns; how lobbies operate; how public opinion works
Facts	Steps in turning bills into laws; how pocket vetoes work; citizens' rights under the Fourteenth Amendment; dominance of federal laws over state laws; constitutional limits on congressional power
Context	Antigay sentiments in Congress and among U.S. population; struggles over finding effective politically correct language; protocols for appropriate interactions with foreign leaders
Insights	Smuggling of contraband is profitable because fines are low compared to gains; tax and other financial incentives can change the labor market, e.g., increase the supply of teachers; governments' power to grant incentives can lead to corruption

information demonstrates how institutions actually work. It makes politics come alive and seem meaningful.

Process information differs significantly from the typical array of facts that news venues tend to favor, such as formal operational rules, the length of officials' terms, formal powers, and how these powers are intended to work. These facts are important, but viewers tend to ignore them, because they usually amount to dry descriptions of governmental issues that casual viewers find very boring. When conventional knowledge tests ask about these kinds of political details, they draw blanks. That leads to verdicts that citizens are ill-informed about politics (Delli Carpini and Keeter, 1996).

Context information in *The West Wing* informs people about the spacious layout of the president's office, its elegant furnishings, and the staff's clothing and body language. It shows how few or how many bodies can fit into this special room.

Insights might relate to tips about graceful ways to dodge a delicate question or refuse an unacceptable request.

Politics in The Sopranos

Whatever cynicism *The West Wing* may lack, *The Sopranos* supplies prodigiously. David Lavery, a professor of English, characterizes the show as profane, blasphemous, scatological, full of wicked humor, brutal, and deeply disturbing (Lavery, 2002). As behooves a story about Mafia types, the tale is short on morality and the action is pervaded by physical violence, racism, sexism, and homophobia. It is loaded with politically incorrect talk and actions, and abounds in norm violations such as openly expressed vicious and insulting comments about African-Americans, Asians, women, and religion.

Still, the show sheds important light on the interface of politics and private-life issues that face middle-class American families. Tony Soprano is undoubtedly a mobster who leads a life of crime. But he is also a man who loves his family, and he wants to provide for his wife and children in the best way possible. That means that he must be concerned with life and health insurance issues, inheritance taxes, college costs, legal fees, and the like. All of these concerns fall into the realm of public policy. Citizens should be aware of them and monitor how their governments deal with them.

Table 4.2 samples political information available from *The Sopranos*.

Politics in The Simpsons

Springfield, U.S.A., where the Simpsons live, like sociologists' Middletown, U.S.A., is the prototype for small-town America and the many problems that these communities face.[2] Sociologists Stephen Scanlan and Seth Feinberg call the show "a microcosm of mainstream American society" (Scanlan and Feinberg, 2000: p. 127). English professor Paul Cantor says it "offers some of the most sophisticated comedy and satire ever to appear on American television" (Cantor, 1999: p. 734). The show depicts major social institutions in operation, starting with the family and moving on

Table 4.2 *The Sopranos* Information Samples

Information Types	Examples
Process	How people hide money overseas to shield it from taxation; how people buy real estate through shell companies to defraud HUD; creating trusts for children; how poor people get free legal services
Facts	History of right to vote in U.S.; history of slavery in U.S.; history of Columbus and Columbus Day; current laws about drug possession and use; First Amendment rights of American citizens
Context	Prevalence of various forms of gambling in recreational facilities; rules of conduct within the mob hierarchy and how they are enforced; continuous police and FBI surveillance of mob activities
Insights	Crooked police cooperate with mobsters to protect gambling; mobsters use prison phones to conduct business; communities have suicide-prevention hotlines; abortion can lead to permanent infertility

to schools, mass media, local government institutions, and the economy.

Springfield's citizens need to address controversial political issues, such as opposition to immigration, legalization of casino gambling, corporate downsizing, and a teacher's strike organized to protest cuts in school funding. Many of these issues are developed in sufficient depth so that viewers can assess the roots of political problems, the reasons for controversy, and the mixed consequences of various solutions. As Cantor explains, "Paradoxically, it is the farcical nature of the show that allows it to be serious in ways that many other television shows are not" (Cantor, 1999: p. 734).

The fact that the show has attracted huge audiences for nearly 20 years proves that it tells stories that resonate with sizable segments of the public. Somewhat surprisingly, it also receives high ratings from teenagers. Like other popular dramas, *The Simpsons* has inspired the formation of online groups of fans who discuss various aspects of the show, including some of its political topics, on message boards. Nightly television news programs rarely elicit such audience participation.

Table 4.3 samples political information available from *The Simpsons.*

Politics in ER

As in all television dramas and situation comedies, the characters in *ER* have interesting personal lives, including romantic relationships. But that does not keep the show from also shedding light on many timely political questions. Examples are the legality of transplanting organs supplied by HIV-positive donors, the problems raised by treating perpetrators and victims of hate crimes, and the steps required to resolve contests over child adoptions when a

Table 4.3 *The Simpsons* Information Samples

Information Types	Examples
Process	How consumer safety is poorly protected; how police act stupidly and engage in sophomoric misbehavior; how public officials excuse their failures; how immigration laws are enforced; how the parole-granting process actually works
Facts	Facts about politics of Hitler, Nixon, Clinton; defendants in lawsuits are innocent until proven guilty; age limits and other rules on gambling; facts about witness-relocation programs; prevalence of gun accidents
Context	Gender role assignments are silly stereotypes; children relish TV cruelty and imitate it; public agencies give preferred treatment to influential people; false values underline hero worship of sports figures
Insights	Regulated industries buy approvals from inspectors; no law forbids written threats; homeowners can fight intruders by violent means; legalized gambling solves a community's financial problems

mother who died was in a same-sex relationship. *ER* has also aired problems presented by violent patients in emergency rooms, the escalating trafficking in human beings, and the challenges posed to the international community by massive casualties sustained in bloody civil wars in Africa.

It is unlikely that most viewers of *ER* will go to the trouble of exploring such issues by consulting regular news sources, which probably would not cover most of them. It is equally unlikely that audiences will fail to learn from the show that these problems currently exist, that they are important for many segments of the public, and that there are no ideal, noncontroversial solutions.

Table 4.4 presents examples of the types of information found in the *ER* episodes that we analyzed for the interview study.

Table 4.4 *ER* Information Samples

Information Types	Examples
Process	The impact of malpractice suits and their settlement on medical care; how hospitals deal with child, spouse, and elder abuse cases; problems of rendering adequate service to patients lacking insurance; how paramedics function
Facts	Parent notification rules about their teens' pregnancies; child custody and adoption rules; legal rights of abuse victims; presurgery consent requirements; do not resuscitate rules
Context	Urban gang problems that generate interpersonal violence; hospital overcrowding that requires premature discharges; need for Spanish-speaking hospital personnel; prevalence of AIDS patients
Insights	Drug addicts may fake injuries to get drugs; Viagra can cause heart failure; asbestos in buildings endangers health; medical ethics prohibits doctors from disclosing patient information to outsiders

The Interviews in Context

To study learning from such shows, we completed a total of 171 interviews in the United States, the Netherlands, and Greece in roughly equal proportions. Here, we concentrate on general conclusions that emerge from the U.S. data.

In addition to interpreting the general messages conveyed by the interviews, we also scrutinized up to six message boards for each of our shows. Message boards allow viewers to post their personal reactions to a particular show and solicit responses from fellow watchers.

To explore how much the stories presented in serial prime-time dramas penetrate American political culture and are therefore likely to increase the show's impact on viewers and nonviewers, we also searched LexisNexis archives for regular news stories that had appeared outside the papers' entertainment section. We looked for stories that mentioned the names of our shows and commented about their political messages or linked them to real-world events. We found a large number of such stories. In fact, the names of shows like *The Sopranos* and *The Simpsons* are often used symbolically to stand for brazen criminal acts or overly simplistic reactions. Jack Bauer's name, featured in *24*, has become a symbol for the view that torture of enemies is permissible if it is used to prevent impending harm (Tenenboim-Weinblatt, 2009).

Did our respondents learn politically useful information from the television dramas that they watched? Answering that question requires defining what we mean by *learn* and *politically useful*. We construe both concepts broadly.

Learning goes beyond gaining totally new information. It also includes broadening and deepening existing knowledge through viewing, or even hearing about, situations that make concepts more real and meaningful. For example, a person may learn from formal schooling or news reports that major American cities have neighborhoods where poverty is rampant and crime thrives. But visiting a slum actually or vicariously via television is a broadening, more graphic experience, which teaches things that words alone cannot completely convey. Actually viewing an event is much more palpable and emotion-stirring than merely hearing or reading about it.

Politically useful means information that helps people understand how and why political issues arise and what consequences they might have. It contributes to the fund of knowledge that this book refers to as the *civic IQ.*

Careful analysis of the conversations embedded in the totality of each interview and in the message board postings firmly supports the important conclusion that regular watching of popular television dramas leads to some kinds of learning that boosts people's understanding of their political world. Learning may be extensive or minor, but it represents measurable gains in understanding. These gains are noticeable, even when the interviews are done days or weeks after the viewers watched the show.

Responses from Telephone Interviews

So what kind of learning did our respondents glean from the nine shows included in our sample? Table 4.5 lists the topics that our respondents discussed at some length. We grouped them into the same four categories as described earlier in this chapter.

Table 4.5 Samples of Learning Reported in Interviews

Information Types	Examples
Process	How the president and Congress work together; how the different branches of government interact; how people are picked for government jobs; how acts of individuals can cause international incidents; how the school voucher system works; how FBI and counterterrorism units interact; relations between top- and bottom-level officials; the problems of women government employees in male-dominated agencies; provision of health care for indigents; honor codes and killings in Middle Eastern societies; problems posed by lack of regulation of Internet content; government agencies' responses in aviation and railroad crashes; living conditions in African refugee camps

Table 4.5 (continued)

Information Types	Examples
Facts	Tools and techniques used in crime detection; U.S. policy on negotiating with terrorists; prerequisites for impeaching a president; sick-leave rights of employed parents; legal limits on the duration of physicians' hospital shifts; inheritance rights when the deceased has left no will; patients' medical privacy rights; carnivals' liability for unsafe rides; individual actions (e.g., a politically motivated assassination) can have systemwide consequences (e.g., provoke war)
Context	Prevalence of subtle racism; the second-class status of AIDS victims; problems of privacy invasion; the power of judges over citizens' personal lives; the amorality of foreign-policy decisions; informal discussions about space exploration; environmental pollution issues; faith versus science discussions
Insights	How to survive a bomb explosion; how to create government in a wilderness setting; use of CPR and other emergency rescue procedures; how to deal with stressed-out coworkers; how to secure a government loan for college

Responses from Message Boards

We report our findings from the Internet message boards separately from the telephone interview findings on the slightly dubious assumption that most message board postings are completely spontaneous, primed or prompted purely by the show. By contrast, findings from the interviews, despite our efforts to keep the situation natural and the messages spontaneous, cannot totally avoid a more or less distinct taint from the interview process.

Our data did show that there is somewhat less variety in the topics of the message board postings than in the interviews, because the message board postings constitute a continuous conversation that clusters around a limited number of topics. One person starts to post comments about a particular topic, and others respond to the initial comment.

Message board conversations may be enlightening, so that participants gain new insights and information. The fact that posted messages repeat information from the show is apt to embed it more firmly in the discussants' minds.

Unlike the comments of message board contributors, the comments of our interviewees are not connected. Since each show represents a smorgasbord of diverse topics, each viewer samples whatever seems most palatable. Collectively, a larger array of topics comes to the fore.

Table 4.6 records our message board findings, again grouped into the four broad categories that reflect the different learning consequences that are likely to be generated. The examples represent politically relevant comments made by three or more individuals, rather than just one person. Table 4.6 combines information from the message boards of different shows. These sites serve demographically diverse audiences. Nonetheless, the posting patterns are quite similar.

Table 4.6 Excerpts from Message Board Findings

Information Types	Examples
Process	Steps to take and organizations to notify if you learn about a terrorist plot against the U.S.; the impact of news stories varies depending on how journalists spin them; police are not used to dealing with deaf people and often misinterpret signing as aggression—police then mistreat them, especially when the deaf person is African-American
Facts	U.S. presidents violate the law if they order assassination of a foreign leader; the Twenty-Fifth Amendment can be used to remove the president from office; there is no system to punish world leaders for their misdeeds; people who get roughed up by police can sue them for brutal behavior; spouses cannot be forced to testify against each other, but may volunteer

Table 4.6 (continued)

Information Types	Examples
Context	All policies entail losses, and citizens must consider that and anticipate and accept some losses for every success; the U.S. never negotiates with terrorists, because that would open the country to future attacks; people assume that public hospitals are inferior in quality to private hospitals, hence they avoid going to public hospitals whenever possible
Insights	The end may justify the means: "If [President] Logan's actions (despicable though they are) result in saving a hundred thousand American lives … well … I would support him … I would sing his praises"; "… it bothers me when the characters sacrifice several civilian lives to save several more … I could see myself being one of the people government decides has to be sacrificed for the greater good (screw the greater good … I want to live damn it … kill everybody else)"; a ballpoint pen can be used for a tracheotomy; AIDS treatments can be jump-started by giving the patient malaria

The Quality of the News Diet

To counteract the impression that the sample information sketched out in Tables 4.5 and 4.6 indicates that audiences of serial television dramas received a sharply limited view of the political world, Table 4.7 presents the full range of subjects covered by the combination of all of our content-analyzed television dramas except *The West Wing* in the weeks prior to the U.S. interviews.

We omitted data from *The West Wing* to avoid overloading the table with information drawn from this explicitly political drama. Like Table 3.1 (in Chapter Three), which summarizes what citizens can learn from entertainment shows, Table 4.7 is organized in topical order; however, the topical arrangements differ to better reflect the characteristics of the information on which our interviews were based. Our interviews did not specifically tap into all of these topic areas, making it impossible to judge the full scope of respondents' learning about them. Self-reports and answers to questions, like flashlights in the dark, conceal more than they reveal.

Table 4.7 A Smorgasbord Menu of Political Information

Topic Areas	Examples
Public policies	Oil wells in Alaska; referenda on school policies; universal health insurance; immigration control; welfare issues; tax fairness
Citizens' rights	Mandatory disclosures about contracts; right to be informed about medical procedures; right to custody of biological children
Public opinions	Acceleration of antiwar feelings; pressures to support government policies as patriotism; anti-Arab sentiments
Public officials	Complexity of jobs; stupidity in decisions; evidence of corruption and favoritism; red tape; agency jurisdiction limits
Lifestyle issues	Gender roles; protecting children in their homes; adoption by stereotyped groups like gays and lesbians; privileges of the rich
Health care issues	Safety of surgeries and drugs; hospital overcrowding; treatment of drug addicts; patient privacy; bad doctors
History topics	Nixon's ouster; Clinton impeachment scenarios; Vietnam war; 1930's Depression; birth of communist China; the Cold War
Family law issues	Premarital arrangements; wills and child custody plans; divorce issues; teenage pregnancy termination; rental deposits
Constitutional provisions	Essential provisions of the First, Fourth, Fourteenth, and Twenty-Fifth Amendments; reasons for constitutional protections; primacy of the Constitution
Role of public agencies	Food and Drug Administration (FDA); Federal Bureau of Investigation (FBI); Coast Guard; Federal Emergency Management Agency (FEMA)
Criminal justice	Activities of prosecutors; lawyers' strategies; public defenders' roles; witnesses' obligations; defendants' strategies; prisons
Group interaction	Need for laws to regulate human interactions; pervasiveness of power struggles; importance of interpersonal relations in politics

It seems fair to argue that citizens deserve to be called *politically alert* when they collectively, albeit not necessarily individually, concern themselves with situations that are encompassed by this broad array of topics. They may not be able to spout numbers about how many of their fellow citizens lack health insurance. They may be unable to recite the names of agencies that deal with terrorist sleeper cells. Nonetheless, collectively as contributors to public opinion, they display real insights about the serious consequences involved in these situations and about the difficulties their government faces in dealing with them. That type of knowledge is valuable for the civic health of the nation and cause for modest optimism about the civic IQ scores of average Americans and of the American public as a whole.

Our interviews and message board evidence clearly demonstrate that our television dramas are sources for gaining important knowledge about politics.

Measurement Conundrums

The art and science of measuring human behavior poses countless tricky problems. We wrestled with assessing passive learning, estimating fiction's impact compared to facts, and weighing the political consequences when dramas become news topics.

The Elusiveness of Passive Learning

Most learning from fictional television dramas is unintended, purely passive, and almost entirely unnoticed and therefore unappreciated by viewers as well as observers. The fact that nearly all viewers fail to realize that they are gaining important political insights from their show means that much of the political content is rarely acknowledged when viewers talk with others about the show.

When we monitored conversations in sports bars on nights when dramas were shown, it confirmed that conversations about the show focused primarily on the substance of the plots and on speculations about what might happen in subsequent episodes.

There were relatively few comments about the contexts. We believe that it was largely taken for granted, because all of the guests at the sports bar tables had seen the same contextual elements and were familiar with the symbols through which producers evoke impressions. For example, a run-down house along an unpaved street means "poor neighborhood"; a smiling child eating an ice cream cone signifies innocent "happiness" (Edelman, 1985).

It is interesting that many viewers claimed that they had learned nothing from the shows when we raised the issue at the start of the interview. In the course of the interview, their responses made it quite clear that they had indeed learned from the show. At the conclusion of the interview, some respondents chose to explicitly acknowledge that their initial assessment had been wrong. A few said that they had construed "learning about politics" as memorization of assorted facts.

The Fiction Factor

To what extent is learning deterred by knowledge that prime-time television dramas are fiction? The answer seems to be that most people consider the lines between fiction and reality as quite porous. They believe that fiction mimics reality and what is reported as reality often turns out to be partially or wholly fiction (Yoshimine and Tokosumi, 1999; Green et al., 2002, 2004; Gendler and Kovakovich, 2005). Scholars agree: "The traditional distinctions between news and entertainment content are no longer very helpful" (Mutz, 2001: p. 231; Mutz and Nir, 2010).

Many Americans, especially younger age groups, are skeptical about traditional news programs and regard satirical or fictional news as closer to the truth (Graber, 2009). On a scale that runs from total reality to total fiction, national news broadcasts and television serial dramas are moving ever closer together in the public's estimations.

Our respondents reacted to questions about the concerns they might have when information is presented in fictional settings mostly by saying that the fiction aspect did not matter in terms of taking the situations seriously. In fact, many said that the episodes were very realistic and often more accurate than "real" news. A few went so far as saying that the information was more persuasive as fiction than as real news because the truth criterion was attenuated. No believability tests or other cautions were required. Their fictional friends were more real than the cardboard characters they met in news reports, and they could accept them as friends without worries about the consequences.

At the opposite end of the believability spectrum, a few viewers were very skeptical, claiming that nothing was believable in a fictional event. Some said they accepted the on-screen events as realistic only after checking them against actual events or carefully weighing their plausibility. The typical ambivalence of distrusting fiction yet accepting parts of it nonetheless is typified by a message board post that read, "I find the Dafur (*sic*) storylines watered down. Then I remember I am watching a TV show & need to learn about Dafur (*sic*) via another avenue if I am going to take it like I should. Otherwise it is minimized like so many genocides/ ethnic cleanings that have occurred thru the generations. Sadly, Dafur (*sic*) is not the first man-inflicted tragedy yet very sad to see it happening in 2006" (*ER* chat room).

Dramas as News Topics in Traditional News

People's realization that there is a strong connection between fictional politics and real-life politics is likely to be enhanced by the fact that traditional media often refer to the television shows. For example, the *Chicago Tribune* published an editorial in 2006 celebrating that the paper's choice in *The West Wing*'s presidential election had actually won the election. The editorial expressed chagrin that it would be impossible to gauge if the new president would govern successfully, because the network was discontinuing new episodes of the show.

Even encyclopedias get into the act. For example, Wikipedia has an entry describing a fictional counterespionage unit featured in *The West Wing, 24,* and other shows. Nearly all of our interviewees—even some who did not watch *24*—knew that the initials CTU stood for Counter Terrorism Unit. Furthermore, Wikipedia actually features detailed information about all of the dramas, as if they were real-life happenings. Wikipedia essays include the contents of specific episodes, along with data about actors who play major roles in the shows.

When dramas are explicitly compared to their real-life counterparts, they occasionally are presented as models that should be followed. For instance, in an article in the *Pittsburgh Post-Gazette,* reporter Sally Kalson, praised *The West Wing* candidates for coming "across as utterly genuine. By contrast, too many real politicians seem to have been hollowed out and stuffed with straw polls by party taxidermists, the better to mouth platitudes devoid of meaning or passion." She concluded that "a glimpse of what a genuine exchange could look like makes what passes for presidential debates in this country even more pale and pathetic by comparison" (Kalson, 2005). Zogby International and MSNBC did an actual snap poll immediately following the fictional show.

Press mentions of shows as reference points illustrate that reporters believe ordinary news consumers will be familiar with the characters and what is happening in their drama lives.

How Dramas Affect Viewers' Thinking

There are many indications that habitual viewers take the information dispensed by their favorite shows quite seriously. For example, when the story line in *ER* described desperate medical conditions in Darfur, the region in Sudan then torn by guerilla civil war, the message boards featured discussions about the appropriateness of American doctors volunteering for service in Darfur. The exchanges were grounded in realistic appraisals of the political situation and its human consequences. As is common, many comments revealed strong emotional reactions to the events pictured on the screen.

Comments from interviewees and from message board postings demonstrate that people ponder the happenings in the dramas. They often openly speculate about hidden meanings and hidden purposes that producers of the shows might have, such as advocating specific environmental policies or laws to safeguard the civil rights of gay people. When viewers suspect ulterior motives for the dramas' plots, they watch episodes closely for possible cues that might support their suspicions. Some message board contributors also mentioned that selected shows might be trial balloons for testing prospective governmental actions to gauge the public's reaction. They mentioned that they scrutinized the shows for supportive evidence.

The trial balloon issue had been widely debated in 2005 and 2006 when a sequel to *The West Wing* made the news by featuring a capable woman president. Charges abounded that the sequel, *Commander in Chief,* was designed to convince the American public that a woman could be an effective leader of the country. In the process, the drama would pave the way for Hillary Clinton to compete for the presidency. When the show was canceled in 2006, the producers, and even members of Congress, were flooded with appeals to continue the drama and complaints that the cancellation had been politically inspired by interest groups opposed to open-ing the presidential office to women. The whole incident received wide press coverage.

Still more evidence that people think about the dramas and learn from them comes from conversations in which they link events in the dramas to the real world. Their real-life experiences become yardsticks for assessing the fictional happenings.

For instance, when *The Simpsons* showed a dumb person in charge of nuclear safety, viewers expressed worries about whether the actual people who fill these jobs are smart enough. They told us that Mayor Quimby in *The Simpsons* seemed patterned after real-life Massachusetts Senator Edward Kennedy, and they likened calls for impeaching the president in *24* to impeachment calls in the Nixon and Clinton administrations. Their own memories of these events then became the foil for comparing and judging the fictional situation.

When shows depict situations that most people have not experi-enced in real life, such as the aftermath of a criminal assault or the treatment of comatose patients, viewers wonder to what degree the depiction in the television drama is true to life. Generally, they lean toward accepting the dramatic presentation as reasonably accurate (see Table 5.9 in the next chapter).

Finally, people report a variety of situations where shows have provided them with potential behavior models or actually served as behavior models. For example, some viewers of *Lost* claimed that they learned various survival skills that could be lifesaving if they ever survived a plane crash that landed in an uninhabited location. Viewers also report that they used knowledge gained from several different shows to strategize about getting their children into the best colleges, make provisions for child care in case both parents died, or ask lifesaving questions in medical settings. Viewers even compared actual public policies to the policies reflected in the shows. At times, they suggested that the show had better solutions. Effective waste disposal and recycling policies are examples, as well as numerous policies involving reforms of public school systems.

When it comes to a major learning impact—changing opinions based on situations presented in the dramas—most respondents profess to sticking to their own views. They also express pleasure when their views are backed up by the words or behaviors of actors in the show. A viewer of *The West Wing* commented, "I don't think that it has changed my mind on an issue, but I will use it to support how I already feel." A viewer of *The Simpsons* was slightly more open to change: "I bring my experiences to the show and use the information from the show to broaden my perspective, and I try to change my views a little based on how they portray an issue."

Unexplored or Slighted Learning Facets

Interview protocols, even when questioning is open-ended, put only a small area of the respondent's knowledge and feelings into focus. Therefore, it is not surprising that some of the learning that our interviewees and the posters on Internet websites experienced does not fit neatly into the process information, facts, context information, and insights categories depicted in Tables 4.5 and 4.6.

For example, some respondents told us that viewing the shows had changed the thrust of their attitudes or their behaviors. One viewer noted, "I have learned compassion from *ER*. They show you really well how people feel, so that you can empathize."

Another claimed that *Lost* had made her "more aware of things, more observant." Several respondents told us that their shows had sharpened their interest in politics, so that they were paying more attention to regular political news.

The extensive literature on emotional arousal produced by fictional stories weighs in on the side of viewers who say that experiencing fictional life is quite similar to experiencing real life. Emotional arousal is a powerful trigger of human attention in both arenas. When people observe a situation in an aroused state, they are more likely to notice what is happening and to respond to it.

The many emotional-arousal reactions that our interviewees volunteered support these findings. These reactions encompass a wide range of emotions, including love, concern, empathy, and hope, as well as fear, disgust, anger, and hatred (Yoshimine and Tokosumi, 1999; Gendler and Kovakovich, 2005). Viewers report being "upset," "bothered," and "troubled" when someone in the show receives unfair treatment. They are "thrilled," "excited," and "touched" when good things are happening to people they like. They laugh; they cry; they curse. They report dreaming about characters in the story, and having emotional reactions and even outbursts in those dreams.

Viewers also vividly remember emotional episodes for a long time. A few interviewees were remarkably detailed and emotional when they told us about episodes viewed as long as 18 months earlier.

The False Information Challenge

Not all learning produces sound and helpful knowledge. Situations presented in dramas may be misleading or totally wrong, or far more often, respondents may mangle important facts.

For example, some viewers of *24* completely misperceived the FBI's role in fighting terrorism. They did not know the meaning and implications of a *coup d'état* or the preconditions for impeaching a president, even though these terms and conditions were extensively and correctly covered by the show.

Again, the misperception problem must be put into perspective. Incorrect interpretations of facts are also quite common when people get their information from regular political news (Kull et al., 2003). The fault may lie entirely with the viewer, but in many instances, news stories are flawed because the news reporting was inaccurate and imprecise.

Wrong information can do great harm. Inaccurate impressions of situations and their consequences may lead viewers to wrong decisions. As mentioned in Chapter Three, reports about the consequences of the CSI effect amply document the damage that can be done by deceptive information: Jurors fail to convict obviously guilty criminals in cases where evidence collection does not match the unrealistically high standards set in *CSI* dramas.

The power of news stories and fictional dramas to mislead news consumers is limited, however. Our data also tell us that many viewers are alert to the chances of receiving incorrect information. They take all information—fictional as well as real life—with the proverbial grains of salt. Some mentioned that they verified information seen in shows by consulting other information sources to make sure that the dramas had described the situation correctly.

Viewers of *The Simpsons* often noted that the images of class differences presented in the show are exaggerated along several dimensions. Although exaggerated, these discrepancies get them to ponder about the real nature of class differences.

When *The West Wing* featured important presidential decisions, several viewers commented that real-life presidents consult a far wider circle of advisors than their *West Wing* counterpart. But they could not estimate the actual size of the president's circle of advisors.

Regular newscasts contain similar distortions, because stories about complex events, out of necessity, are stripped of much of the context that would clarify the full meaning of the situation. Viewers keep such distortions in mind, just as they do for fictional shows. Some viewers contend that fictional shows can come closer to the realities of life because they have more time to tell their audiovisual tales than is the case for print and television news stories.

Sharing Human Experiences

The overall impressions about lessons that emerge from the interviews with American respondents most likely apply to audiences in other cultures as well, because they reflect human behavior in general. The fact that great fiction and nonfiction books, theater performances, operas, and television shows can attract millions of people living in divergent cultures is proof that dramas about human experiences have universal appeal.

Of course, there are discordances in reactions as well. Some spring from multiple versions of the dramas designed to accommodate cultural taboos. For example, many American television serial dramas that are exported to Middle Eastern countries are edited to remove explicit sexual themes likely to offend Islamic religious traditions. Other reactions are divergent simply because audiences come from different cultural backgrounds.

What similarities and what differences would become apparent when we dissected the responses of interviewees from the United States, the Netherlands, and Greece? Chapter Five tells that story. It also sketches out how differences in political backgrounds and in traditions and experiences account for the response differences that we observed.

CHAPTER FIVE
LEARNING FROM TELEVISION DRAMAS

WHAT EUROPEANS TOLD US

with Tereza Capelos

Luck sometimes strikes unexpectedly and brings rich rewards. When I casually discussed the findings of the American interviews with a colleague during a visit to the University of Leiden in the Netherlands, she offered to undertake a parallel study with Dutch viewers. That companion study would shed light on similarities and differences in political learning when viewers are steeped in different political cultures. She thought that a colleague in Greece would also be interested in this question and eager to do a parallel study with Greek citizens.

And so it happened. Dr. Tereza Capelos, the primary author of this chapter, then teaching at the University of Leiden and now at the University of Surrey, generated the interviews in the Netherlands and Greece. The Dutch data were collected with the help of a research team lead by Leiden graduate student Sander Ensink. The Greek companion data were collected with the help of Professor Nicolas Demertzis, at the University of Athens, and Leiden graduate student Kostantinos Vadratsikas, who also assisted with the qualitative content analysis of the interviews.

The efforts of these scholars are an immensely important step in fathoming how messages that crisscross national boundaries more or less continuously in our globalized society are understood by people steeped in vastly varied political experiences. My American assistants and I are exceedingly grateful for the significant contributions made to this book by our European colleagues.

The Impact of Sociopolitical and Cultural Factors

This chapter puts the findings from the interviews under the microscope. When we listen to the interviews, what do they tell us about entertainment television's impact on the civic IQ of viewers in the Netherlands and Greece? How do the European findings compare with the findings from the United States?

We want to focus especially on the impact of cross-cultural factors on learning, because meaning construction requires blending incoming information with information that each viewer already holds in memory. We naturally expect that people in Greece bring different political experiences to the table than people living in the Netherlands or the United States. There are many similarities in the political environments of the three countries, but there are also significant differences.

One important belief shared by the three cultures is that entertainment television is exactly what the category name suggests: entertainment and nothing more. It is a pleasurable diversion from the grim realities of life.

Fictional television dramas, unlike life, do not require intensive learning. Aside from embedding the details of the story in memory, so that you can follow the chain of events and talk about them with others, the information contained in the story is inconsequential. Therefore, when people are asked whether they have encountered useful political information in fictional television dramas, the quick and easy stereotypical response is a resounding "No."

Clichéd answers are common in interviews, given the power of stereotypes to dominate thinking. Therefore, the interview results reported in this chapter must be interpreted in light of the strength of prevailing clichés and stereotypes.

The data reported in the tables in this chapter must also be weighed in terms of an average person's learning behavior. When people encounter a smorgasbord of political information from which they can choose or abstain at will, most consume very little. Precise percentages are elusive, but less than 10 percent of the audience of an average television newscast pays serious attention to any one of the political stories (Graber, 2007). In the apt words of political scientist W. Russell Neuman, "[M]ost political learning is fragmentary, haphazard and incidental. The citizen ... picks up bits and pieces of information over time, gradually accumulating a composite picture of the prominent issues ... " (Neuman, 1986: p. 136, 156). Compared to learning from regular nonfiction news offerings, the rates of learning from fictional television dramas are quite impressive, even though the percentage numbers are low.

Television dramas, because of their potential to reach millions, provide individuals with common frames of reference (Sachleben and Yeneral, 2004). While the main purpose for watching television dramas is entertainment, audiences nonetheless obtain information about political, economic, and social matters. Viewers then use this information to make comparisons with the institutions and services of their own country. In this sense, watching American-produced television dramas enhances the European audiences' ability to understand political life, inside and outside their country's borders.

The story lines of the shows create opportunities to draw parallels with political persons and institutions at home and abroad. Opportunities for learning about American politics are ample in the Netherlands and Greece because both countries have a high rate of imported programming from the United States. The imports are presented in their original format and language, with subtitles in the local language. This format preserves the original character of the shows and enhances English language learning. English comprehension is quite high in both countries.

A Thumbnail View of the European Settings

Viewers in Greece and the Netherlands differ in what they learn and how they view information in the shows. In many instances, these dissimilarities reflect differences in the political, cultural, and media systems of the two countries. The Netherlands and Greece are both small, European countries.[1]

The Netherlands Setting

The Netherlands is a parliamentary democracy and constitutional monarchy, with high voter participation across the adult population and only small differences in turnout across different age groups (Wattenberg, 2003). Citizens of the Netherlands enjoy a high standard of living, and they consistently display robust scores in cross-national comparisons on civic literacy. The segment of the population that ranks at the bottom end of the scale of civic literacy is tiny and significantly smaller than in most European countries. These admirable statistics are attributed to the information-rich environment available to the Dutch. They enjoy an excellent educational system, have access to high-quality news programming on public television, and display high levels of newspaper readership.

The quality of television programming is a consequence of the strong public television tradition of the Netherlands. Commercial broadcasting was legalized in 1988. At the start of the twenty-first century, seven large television stations, and numerous specialized stations, were in operation (Brants, 2004). As a result, the media diet of Dutch viewers is rich and diverse. While newspaper readership is overall in decline, the Netherlands displays a higher per-capita average readership of newspapers than most European countries. In short, to keep up-to-date with public affairs, the average citizen in the Netherlands is accustomed to relying on excellent news and a high standard of programming.

The Greece Setting

Turning to Greece, we can identify several points of departure from the Dutch political and cultural environment. In the Greek parliamentary republic, voting is compulsory, with turnout reaching more than 70 percent of the total electorate.

Despite the high participation rates in elections, the Greek political culture is stained by the absence of a strong civil society and the high level of distrust for, and dissatisfaction with, political institutions and actors (Lyrintzis, 1984; Mouzelis, 1980, 1995; Tsoukalas, 1981; Demertzis, 1994; Sotiropoulos, 1995). Political and social interactions are tarred by favoritism, patronage, and corruption, compromising trust and other forms of social capital.

Individualism and family-oriented values dominate the Greek society. The lack of shared interests and values deters the development of an empowered watchdog-oriented citizenry (Sotiropoulos and Karamagioli, 2006). In addition, despite the high level of literacy, the civic IQ fluctuates considerably. The segment of citizens that fall into the bottom group of civic literacy is much larger in Greece than in the Netherlands (Milner, 1998; European Commission, Eurobarometer 44.2, 2001). Greeks also have low newspaper readership and the lowest proportion of Internet users in the European Union (Papathanasopoulos, 2004).

Turning to the contents of the media diet that Greek citizens are likely to receive, the print media are characterized by the strong presence of a party press, unlike their Dutch counterparts. As a result, political news reporting is seldom balanced. It usually carries the political/ideological assessment and interpretation of the editorial team of the newspaper. Electronic media are not much different.

Content analysis of Greek news broadcasts demonstrates the highly dramatized character of news presentation, both on public and private television stations. The news programs share a large number of characteristics with entertainment programming, such as emotive language and high levels of intense conflict.

To recap, audience exposure to American television dramas is high in the Netherlands and Greece. However, the countries differ in their political culture and civic society, public orientations toward political and media institutions, the frequency of consumption, and the format and tone of their news broadcasts. All of these factors play a role in differential learning among the two audiences. As discussed in Chapter Four, the studies that we conducted in the Netherlands and Greece test for these differences by analyzing the interview responses of regular television drama viewers.

How Content Travels Across National Boundaries

The comparative nature of the data allows us to look for variations in patterns of meaning construction. In the pages that follow, we compare what viewers learned in Greece and the Netherlands. We are also interested in whether imported political content stimulates political learning in the same fashion as it does when the shows originate in your home country. To find out, we look for differences in political learning between the American and European viewers.

Variations in Patterns of Meaning Construction

It has long been known that sociopolitical and cultural differences are important factors when it comes to assigning meaning to entertainment shows. The phenomenon has been investigated in the past in Israel in the context of assessing the impact of the television show *Dallas* among Arabs, Russian Jews, Moroccan settlers, and members of kibbutzim (typically second-generation Israelis). Studies have also been done among second-generation Americans in Los Angeles and in Japan (Liebes and Katz, 1990).

Communication professors Tamar Liebes and Elihu Katz found that culturally diverse people watching *Dallas* in Israel, the United States, and Japan emphasized different aspects of the show, while people belonging to the same cultural groups paid attention to similar information. For example, viewers from the United States focused on the soap-opera characters of the show, while the Japanese paid little attention to them. Moroccan viewers in Israel were especially concerned with moral issues and found the show insulting to their values, whereas Russian viewers seemed to be particularly attracted to the political information (Liebes and Katz, 1990).

The Interview Itinerary

Our European interviews focused on eight of the nine American television dramas discussed in Chapter Four: *The Simpsons, Family Guy, CSI, The Sopranos, Grey's Anatomy, ER, Lost,* and *24*. We did not include *The West Wing* because that show was not available to viewers in these countries at the time of the study.

Cold-call telephone interviews were conducted with 69 participants in Greece and 52 in the Netherlands, in addition to 50 participants in the United States, between January 2007 and February 2008 (see Chapter Three for more details).

In Europe, the participants, who were regular viewers of the shows, were selected via a snowball sample, which, like the American sample, depended on soliciting of names of potential subjects.[2] We generated the snowball sample by starting interviews with a few viewers of each show, and then asking the respondents to refer others for participation in the study, who in turn referred still others. Each interview took about 20 minutes and was recorded by telephone-recording equipment, with the consent of the participants. Interviews were then transcribed for analysis. Table 5.1 contains a description of our sample per country and show.

During each interview, the respondents answered questions related to one particular show, even when they had watched more

Table 5.1 Participants per Country

	Greece %	Netherlands %	U.S. %
24	13	0	18
CSI	18.8	22.2	0
ER	20.3	5.8	22
Lost	26.1	3.8	8
The Simpsons	13	17.3	26
Grey's Anatomy	7.2	44.2	20
Sopranos	1.4	5.8	0
Family Guy	0	0	6
Other show	0	1.9	0
Number of responses	69	52	50

than one show. The interviews included general questions for all shows and specific questions for individual shows. In some interviews, some questions were omitted or left unanswered.

As discussed in Chapter Three, the questionnaire contained items that tap into viewers' reasons for watching television dramas, how much they learn, and how they use the political information available in the shows. A set of questions focuses on what viewers learn from watching the shows, exploring whether the information they acquire enhances their ability to understand how real-life politics and institutions function.

To measure the impact of the shows on viewers' civic IQ, European respondents were asked the following:

- Whether the show promoted participation in political discussions and other political activities
- To apply what they had learned to both real-life situations and hypothetical situations
- To compare the fictional situations depicted in the show to real-life situations in their countries

Our analysis of the data focuses on reasons for watching the shows, ranging from entertainment values to knowledge acquisition, the types of information that audiences learn, and the degree to which this information affects their understanding of politics.

Remember that the main reason for watching television dramas is entertainment. Our data, however, show that the viewers of these entertainment programs, which are anchored in contemporary life situations, also receive valuable information about current issues, which helps them understand aspects of their political reality.

To recap, in this chapter, we are interested in how much, in what ways, and what types of political information viewers in Greece and the Netherlands learn from imported television dramas. Although the main reason for watching these dramas is entertainment, we expect that besides their entertainment value, the scenarios depicted in the dramas contribute to viewers' understanding of politics. We anticipate that viewers acquire information passively about political and other issues, and that this information enhances their ability to understand patterns of political life, including insights about how political institutions function. We also expect that most of the messages embedded in these shows will leave only brief impressions, which will fade quickly unless they are reinforced repeatedly.

Reasons for Watching Television Dramas: The Power of Entertainment

In our interviews, we asked open-ended and closed-ended questions. To evaluate the responses, we grouped the reasons for watching the show into categories. We also asked viewers directly whether they had learned anything from the show applicable to their own lives.

Open-Ended Responses

We expected that European viewers, like viewers in the United States, watch television dramas mainly for entertainment; they do not plan to learn from them. To capture the viewers' assessment of the benefits gained from drama viewing, we asked them an open-ended question about their reasons for watching their chosen drama and their evaluation of the benefits. Their answers were diverse and thought-provoking.[3]

Characteristically, a Greek participant who watches *CSI* commented dispassionately about performance features. He said, "The show has short episodes. It is a pleasant way to spend my time. It is interesting and has suspense." A Dutch participant agreed, but emphasized his personal interaction with the show: "I like the puzzles! I try to outsmart the *CSI* team, and I like the stories and the setting. I love justice series. Perhaps this is because I work for the Justice Department."

Similarly, a Dutch viewer of *Grey's Anatomy* noted, "I watch it because it has good actors. I recognize hospital affairs because I am part of it. I see it in my job all the time. The relationships are also intriguing."

Regarding *Lost,* a Greek viewer noted, "It is shot in an exotic place, has an attractive group of young actors. It is well directed, and the story is unpredictable."

Referring to *The Simpsons,* a Dutch participant said, "I watch *The Simpsons* because it gives me an insight in the USA popular culture, and it is critical of society. It offers a satire of its norms and values."

Response Categories

To be able to identify systematic patterns in the interviewee responses, we coded and categorized them using the following categories: excitement, entertainment and relaxation, artistic features, scenarios and formats, practical information, insights and understanding, and other reasons. Table 5.2 presents the results for each of the countries.

As expected, the open-ended self-reports of the Greek, Dutch, and American participants point consistently to entertainment, excitement, and relaxation as the most prominent reasons for watching television dramas. At least half or more of the participants in each country make an entertainment-related reference. In Greece, about 48 percent of the participants mention entertainment. That number rises in the Netherlands to about 67 percent, and tops at 96 percent in the United States.

Table 5.2 Reason for Watching the Show

	Greece %	Netherlands %	U.S. %
Excitement/entertainment/ relaxation	47.6	66.7	96
Artistic features/scenario/ format	28.6	16.7	4
Acquire practical information	12.7	6.3	0
Gain insights/understanding	4.8	10.4	0
Other reasons	6.3	0	0
Number of responses	63	48	50

The artistic features of the show—for example, the direction, photography, scenarios, and acting—are a weak second, with just around 29 percent of the participants in Greece and 17 percent in the Netherlands. In the United States, only 4 percent mention them.

The emphasis on entertainment was no surprise. People often have stock answers about why they engage in certain behaviors or why they make particular choices. These answers are akin to automatic reflexes. When it comes to entertainment television, we expect entertainment to be the first answer that springs to mind when questioned about popular television dramas.

What is astonishing is that the informational value of the shows, either in the form of practical information or as insights, is recognized by a few participants in Greece and the Netherlands; U.S. participants miss it entirely. This prompted us to probe further to uncover the potential educational value of television dramas that are imported from abroad and reflect happenings in foreign settings.

Closed-Ended Responses

To assess the significance of each of the potential reasons for watching a show, we followed up with four closed-ended items. Each question referred to a particular reason for watching the show, and viewers were asked to specify the extent to which this reason applied to them personally. Tables 5.3 through 5.6 present the scores of the closed-ended questions for viewers in the three countries.

Across the board, the highest mean scores refer to relaxation and entertainment (Table 5.3). They range from 7.87 in the case of Greece to 9.73 for U.S. participants. While all score high on the entertainment value of the shows, Greek responses are statistically lower compared with the other two countries. In fact, 88 percent of Dutch and 94 percent of American respondents report that they watch shows for relaxation and entertainment a great deal. In contrast, only 54 percent of Greeks provided the same high response for entertainment, a statement perhaps of their general dissatisfaction with the standards of television programming in their country.

Table 5.3 Watch the Show for Relaxation and Entertainment (Closed-Ended)

	Greece %	Netherlands %	U.S. %
Not at all	4.3	0	0
A little	8.7	0	2
Somewhat	33.3	12.2	4.1
A great deal	53.6	87.8	93.9
Number of responses	69	49	49
Mean (standard deviation)	7.87[a] (2.74)	9.60[b] (1.10)	9.73[b] (1.15)

Next to the mean, the value in parentheses reports standard deviation. Common superscripts (a, b) indicate nonsignificant mean differences at the 0.05 level. The range of the variable is on a 0 to 10 scale, where 0 represents not at all and 10 a great deal.

Socializing receives the second highest score as a reason for watching the shows in the closed-ended responses (Table 5.4). Here, U.S. average scores reach a high of 7.13 points, stressing the social capital value of the shows. Connecting with family and friends is also an important function of the shows in Greece, where the mean score is 4.02 points, while it is not as important in the Netherlands, where the average score is a low of 2.81 points. Characteristically, about 47 percent of the American participants find the socializing value of the show to be of great importance.

Table 5.4 Watch the Show to Connect with Family and Friends (Closed-Ended)

	Greece %	Netherlands %	U.S. %
Not at all	20.6	45.1	14.0
A little	48.5	33.3	4.7
Somewhat	20.6	13.7	34.9
A great deal	10.3	7.8	46.5
Number of responses	69	51	43
Mean (standard deviation)	4.02[a] (2.97)	2.81[b] (3.15)	7.13[c] (3.46)

Next to the mean, the value in parentheses reports standard deviation. Common superscripts (a, b, c) indicate nonsignificant mean differences at the 0.05 level. The range of the variable is on a 0 to 10 scale, where 0 represents not at all and 10 a great deal.

On the other hand, about 45 percent of the Dutch participants do not see any socializing value in watching these television dramas.

These thought-provoking differences suggest that watching entertainment television serves different purposes across countries. Where these shows have been on the air for years, as in the United States, they have generated loyal audiences who get together to watch, enjoy, and discuss them. They become a significant staple of social relations, and are recognized as such. Where the shows have been broadcast for only a few years, these practices have not yet developed to a significant extent.

Turning to other reasons for watching the shows, in Tables 5.5 and 5.6, we see that information-related goals, such as gaining practical information and insights, ranked low overall. When asked directly (Table 5.5), close to 59 percent of Dutch participants and 64 percent of U.S. participants see absolutely no practical value in television dramas.

Similarly, in Table 5.6, when respondents were asked if they watch the show for information and insights, about 55 percent of the Dutch participants and 53 percent of the American participants answered not at all. These answers are in line with viewers' stereotypical perceptions of the value of the shows, and therefore are not surprising.

Table 5.5 Watch the Show for Advice or Opinions About Practical Matters (Closed-Ended)

	Greece %	Netherlands %	U.S. %
Not at all	34.8	58.8	63.9
A little	34.8	29.4	16.7
Somewhat	23.2	11.8	19.4
A great deal	7.2	0	0
Number of responses	69	51	36
Mean (standard deviation)	3.43[a] (3.13)	1.77[b] (2.34)	1.85[b] (2.89)

Next to the mean, the value in parentheses reports standard deviation. Common superscripts (a, b) indicate nonsignificant mean differences at the 0.05 level. The range of the variable is on a 0 to 10 scale, where 0 represents not at all and 10 a great deal.

Table 5.6 Watch the Show for Insights (Closed-Ended)

	Greece %	Netherlands %	U.S. %
Not at all	29.0	55.1	53.1
A little	36.2	36.7	12.5
Somewhat	27.5	8.2	28.1
A great deal	7.2	0	6.3
Number of responses	69	49	32
Mean (standard deviation)	3.77[a] (3.07)	1.77[b] (2.16)	2.92[ab] (3.46)

Next to the mean, the value in parentheses reports standard deviation. Common superscripts (a, b) indicate nonsignificant mean differences at the 0.05 level. The range of the variable is on a 0 to 10 scale, where 0 represents not at all and 10 a great deal.

What is noteworthy is the difference across countries. As the mean scores in Tables 5.5 and 5.6 show, Greek viewers paid substantially more attention to the educational values of the dramas than their Dutch and American counterparts. Previous tables indicated that the entertainment value of the shows was overall lower for Greek viewers. We think this trend reflects differences in the character of news broadcasts.

In Greece, the types of information viewers receive via news broadcasts is highly emotive and dramatized. Viewers therefore do not draw clear lines between entertainment programming and informational programming. Television dramas, like news programs, become sources of insights and practical tips, not just relaxation.

On the other hand, where news programming is dispassionate and objective, as in the Netherlands, the viewers rarely claim that the shows guide their opinions or provide useful insights. The responses of U.S. participants were similar, though not identical.

Personal Usefulness of Information

Our last direct learning question was whether viewers had learned anything from the show that they could use in their own lives. As expected, the instinctive responses were negative.

Characteristically, a Greek participant said about *24,* "No, there isn't something new to learn." Another Greek viewer of *ER* noted,

"I couldn't learn because I am not a doctor. The show gives lots of information about medical issues that I didn't understand anyway."

But there were positive responses as well. A Greek respondent discussing *24* made a reference to practical information: "Yes, I learned something—to buy a PDA with a GPS." A Dutch viewer of *Grey's Anatomy* noted, "Yes, like with Christina and Burke—it is quite realistic that people can react in such a way, and you start to think about how you would deal with someone who reacts like this. But these are small things. It is mostly a drama series." A Greek *ER* viewer acknowledged, "Yes, I learn how things are in a USA hospital."

We recoded all of the answers on the basis of the content and the type of learning that occurred using the following categories: nothing, insights on human relations and behavior, practical information, institutions and procedures, and other. Table 5.7 shows that about 55 percent of the Dutch respondents and 50 percent of the American respondents failed to identify anything that they learned from the show. But only 39 percent of the Greek viewers gave a negative response. Table 5.7 shows that a goodly number of viewers do recall learning information from watching TV dramas, although they are at first loathe to admit it.

Respondents' recall of clearly political content, recorded in the institutions and procedures category, is limited to 4 to

Table 5.7 Is there anything you have learned from the show that you can use in your life?

	Greece %	Netherlands %	U.S. %
Nothing	39.1	54.8	50
Insights on human relations/ behavior	29.7	26.2	12
Practical information	21.9	11.9	24
Institutions and procedures	4.7	4.8	4
Other	3.1	2.4	10
Not sure/can't remember	1.6	0	0
Number of responses	64	42	50

almost 5 percent in each country. About 30 percent of the Greek respondents and 26 percent of the Dutch focused on insights regarding human relations and behavior. This number was much lower among U.S. participants (about 12 percent). The explanation may be that individual-level interactions among Americans, depicted in U.S.-produced dramas, may surprise foreign viewers accustomed to different types of relationships and norms of individual behavior. Unfamiliarity may make these interactions more memorable.

For the U.S. participants, these interactions are not noteworthy. They show a preference for practical information (24 percent) instead. Practical information is also high on the list of Greek participants (about 22 percent). A Greek viewer of *ER* noted, "I learned information about appendicitis." Another Greek viewer of the same show said, "Well, in one episode, someone had high fever, and they took him out in the snow. That means that if you do something with cold water, you will save him."

Because respondents often give answers on the basis of what they think the answer should be, we explored the degree and content of their learning beyond these closed-ended questions and asked several open-ended questions that tap into the information recalled from the shows. The fact that respondents used their own words to elaborate on what they remembered from the shows gave us additional opportunities to identify what grabbed their attention and what types of information they deemed important. We then followed up with specific questions in order to investigate the reasons for recalling particular pieces of information and viewers' trust in the accuracy of the information they drew from the shows.

Evidence of Learning from TV Dramas

To find evidence of learning from these shows, we asked open-ended questions. We classified the responses into categories that indicated the nature of knowledge gains. We also asked the viewers about the credibility of television dramas compared to standard news programs.

Open-Ended Responses

First, we asked participants to explain briefly what happened in the last episode they had watched of their favorite show. Strikingly, despite the variation in the types of information they remembered, all participants had ample specific knowledge about the content. For the majority, this knowledge focused on the action and the plot, as well as the relationships among the characters.

Describing *Lost,* a Greek participant remembered, "Well, it was about Jack, Kate, and Sawyer. They were trapped in a village and were trying to escape." A Dutch viewer of *Grey's Anatomy* recalled, "Meredith tells two men that she is dating both of them. They then try to outclass each other." Discussing *The Simpsons,* a Dutch participant remembered, "Homer stuffs his face in order to qualify for a government home-repair grant," and a Greek viewer noted, "Homer declared his house an independent state!"

We then asked respondents *why* they thought they remembered the particular information. Some viewers referred to interesting or impressive qualities of the plot. For example, one Greek viewer, commenting on *Lost,* said, "I remember details because I like shows that have something metaphysical. This is also what attracted my interest to continue watching." Regarding *The Simpsons,* a Dutch viewer mentioned the entertainment value of the story: "I remember it because it was a very funny episode, and it connects with my personal sense of humor."

However, that was not the whole story. In fact, several viewers diverted from the standard entertainment-related responses and offered reasons pointing to gaining insights about particular situations. One Greek viewer of *Lost* noted, "I remember it because it demonstrates common human behavior." Another Greek viewer discussing *The Simpsons* said, "It is memorable because it shows the truth about our times and how people are indifferent."

Types of Learning

We also classified the open-ended answers according to the kind of information that they had provided for each viewer. Had they referred to minor or major facts? Did they involve evaluations, new slants on facts or relationships, or vicarious experiences, or did they merely refresh fading memories?

An example of learning new slants on facts comes from a Greek viewer of *ER*: "Watching this show, I learned a lot about the way they deal with patients. Also how important communication is." Referring to the show *24*, another Greek viewer provided an example of evaluations by stating, "I learned how important strong family bonds are." An example of learning additional facts came from the *ER* viewer who said, "I learned how and when one can perform a tracheotomy." A Dutch viewer of *Lost* mentioned, "I learned survival techniques on a deserted island." Referring to an episode that described a traffic accident, a Greek *ER* viewer recalled existing memories: "I have seen some things that I already knew and I have seen them in real life, too."

Table 5.8, which aggregates all responses across the three countries, reveals some interesting patterns. First, we note that learning occurs more often as enrichment of existing knowledge, while learning something completely new is less frequent. This is a familiar pattern for adults, because they use the mental schemas stored in their memories as guides for acquiring compatible new information.

Specifically, about 39 percent of Greek respondents reported having learned additional minor facts, and about 46 percent of their

Table 5.8 Usage of Learning Categories

	Greece %	Netherlands %	U.S. %
Add minor facts	38.9	5.3	8.3
New slants on facts	19.4	5.3	0
Add evaluations	16.7	5.3	16.7
New slants on relationships	8.3	42.1	4.2
Add experiential insights	8.3	15.8	25.0
Add major facts	5.6	26.3	45.8
Refresh fading memories	2.8	0	0
Number of responses	36	19	24

American counterparts thought that they had learned additional major facts about some current issue. The difference between Greeks and Americans may not be as sharp as it appears, because the boundary between major facts and minor facts is imprecise.

New slants on facts and new facts on relationships received lower ratings from Greeks and Americans. Both groups report learning occasionally about evaluations (about 17 percent) and insights (about 8 percent and 25 percent, respectively).

On the other hand, the Dutch respondents' answers referred much more often to information regarding relationships (about 42 percent) and less often to adding major facts (about 26 percent). This is in line with a point mentioned earlier: The high quality of news programming and the high newspaper readership in the Netherlands satisfy the information appetite of our Dutch respondents. Primarily, they look for facts when they consume news offerings and for entertainment when they watch television dramas. For Greek audiences, the dramatic and often confrontational tone of news programs creates information gaps, and they may use entertainment television to fill in these gaps in their knowledge of facts.

While participants seem to be acquiring particular information from the shows, to what extent are they willing to incorporate it into their knowledge base? Are viewers comfortable with the idea that the information comes from fictional television dramas? In general, the answer is affirmative, although some viewers are more comfortable than others. Greeks are significantly more comfortable, with a score of 8.84 on a 0 to 10 scale. Dutch viewers follow with a 7.38 score, while Americans retain more reservations, scoring 6.26 points. For the Greeks, the borders between entertainment and information are blurred, whereas for Americans, a television drama's primary function is entertainment, and this disqualifies it from being a reliable information source.

Comparing Television Dramas with Traditional News

Our next aim was to probe more deeply into the link between entertainment offerings and information gain. We asked participants how well the credibility of television dramas fared in each country in comparison to traditional news broadcasts. Was information from television dramas less believable when compared to news stories?

Comments sprinkled throughout the interviews suggested that some viewers had doubts about the reliability of the information in the dramas. There were remarks that the show was not real or accurate, that it had an artistic and dramatic format, and that it exaggerated. Other viewers noted that it was impossible to verify information from shows. On the positive side, some viewers apparently had confidence in the accuracy of shows because they believed that experts had participated in writing the script.

Table 5.9 shows that although the majority of respondents in all three countries find information originating from television dramas less believable than the news, about 46 percent of Greek and American participants do not see things as clear-cut. In fact, many of our respondents thought that, under certain conditions, information from television dramas can be as believable as the news.

A Greek viewer of *CSI* noted, "The information in the show is not very serious for such a popular show, but also the press is biased. The show is very close to the truth." A Dutch viewer of *CSI* said, "The producers of the show try to be realistic, yet are forced to shorten evidence-processing time to keep [the] audience."

Other viewers found the story lines less believable than the news because they portray institutions as competent when they do not function well in reality. For example, a Greek viewer of *CSI*, disillusioned with the actions of police in real life, noted, "The show exaggerates.... We hear in the news about such things, but in the show, the policemen act faster and smarter."

Table 5.9 Is information from television dramas less believable than the news?

	Greece %	Netherlands %	U.S. %
Less believable than the news	54.0	73.5	53.3
As believable as the news	19.0	8.2	32.6
It depends	27.0	18.4	14.0
Number of responses	63	49	43

So why is it that some viewers, mainly Greeks and Americans, did not find significant differences between the news and the stories of the television dramas? We think that this statistic speaks directly to the character of news broadcasts in Greece and the United States, where news content is dramatized and framed to appeal to emotions. The Dutch viewers are more likely to distinguish between the format of the fictional dramas and the format of actual news stories. Their views can be understood in the context of the less dramatized, highly respected, and objectively delivered content of news broadcasts in the Netherlands.

Are viewers able to identify changes in their political awareness after watching the dramas? Not surprisingly, when we asked for a yes or no response, about 85 percent of the participants in Greece, 70 percent in the Netherlands, and 69 percent in the United States reported that they found no difference in their levels of political awareness after watching television dramas. Not everyone was equally negative, however.

A minority that ranges from 15 percent in Greece to 26 percent in the Netherlands and 31 percent in the United States say they are more aware of political issues following the dramas. While the numbers are small, they are large in the context of learning that follows from the flood of nonfiction news messages to which average people are normally exposed. Most of these messages are quickly discarded from their short-term memories. By comparison, impact rates of 15 to 31 percent are actually impressive.

Socialization and Mobilization Effects

Civic IQ does not depend primarily on the retention of political facts. As discussed earlier, it involves the integration of political information into citizens' thinking and the use of this information when making political choices.

To examine to what extent television dramas enhance the viewers' civic IQ, we asked our respondents questions relating to political mobilization that might be inspired by the shows. We wanted to know whether watching the shows might inspire viewers to donate money to hospitals or other organizations, to initiate discussions about political topics of interest, or to contact organizations to urge them to take action concerning a political problem.

Behavior Changes

About 26 percent of the American participants reported that they learned something that effectively changed their political behavior. Most European participants (around 95 percent) answered that their political behavior was not affected by the show. A few viewers differed, mentioning changes in political or personal behaviors, or in the potential for change or desire for change.

For example, a Dutch viewer who discussed the effects of *CSI* commented, "The episode was talking about a DNA bank. The show made me a little more fearful, and I am now more critical regarding evidence; there is DNA everywhere." A Greek viewer of *Lost* noted, "I was affected as far as my relations with other people are concerned." And another viewer noted changes in her political behavior: "I donated money for medical purposes." A Greek viewer of *ER* also answered positively: "Yes, my behavior changed. The show prompted me to work for the society. I was sensitized for voluntary work and participation in NGOs [nongovernmental organizations]." A Dutch viewer of *Grey's Anatomy* expressed her desire to change behavior but reported no actual change: "Not so far, but I want to become a donor." And a Greek viewer of *ER* remarked about the potential for behavioral changes: "I have not changed my behavior, but I think that, in general, it can make people more sensitive."

The scarcity of reports of behavioral changes in the European sample suggests that television dramas are more likely to inspire some forms of action in their native sociopolitical environment than when they are imported into other political and cultural settings. In the United States, the effects of television dramas on behaviors are more substantial because the shows often address acute local and national problems. In fact, episodes are often sponsored by government agencies to promote engagement with specific social problems. In the Dutch and Greek cases, the story line might focus attention on particular issues and raise awareness, but the viewers recognize that the shows mainly depict American situations, and not their native political reality.

Personal interactions and conversations are also evidence that the show left an impression on many viewers. With this in mind, we asked respondents if they were alone or with others when they watched the drama and whether they discussed it. We already saw that socializing is a frequently reported reason for watching the dramas—more so in the United States and Greece than in the Netherlands. As shown in Table 5.10, about 56 percent of the American respondents report being with friends when they watch the show. Another 22 percent are with family members, while only 19 percent watch the show alone.

The situation is different for European respondents. Greeks tend to watch the show mainly alone (about 55 percent) or alternatively, with friends. Dutch respondents watch their favorite show alone only 34 percent of the time; watching it with family is their next preference. Remember that it was Greeks who praised the socializing value of watching the show. Yet, they are most likely to watch it alone. The explanation seems to be that the socializing value comes in engaging in conversations about the dramas.

Discussing Drama Episodes

Table 5.11 sheds light on the increased social capital created by television dramas in the United States, where about 63 percent

Table 5.10 Do you watch the show alone or with other people? Who?

	Greece %	Netherlands %	U.S. %
Alone	54.7	34	18.8
With friends	14.1	12	56.3
Sometimes alone or with friends	14.1	24	3.1
Sometimes alone or with family	9.4	4	0
With family	7.8	26	21.9
Number of responses	64	50	32

of respondents report discussing the episode after every showing. In the Netherlands, regular discussions drop to about half of that (around 35 percent), while about 24 percent report that they do not discuss things that happen in the show. In Greece, although most viewers watch the show alone, only about 7 percent report never discussing the show. Discussions among Greek viewers happen mostly occasionally (around 63 percent), rather than regularly (about 29 percent). The comparable figures for Dutch viewers are about 41 and 35 percent.

When discussions take place, information is exchanged. How common is the transmission of information among viewers? About 57 percent of the respondents in Greece, 41 percent in the Netherlands, and 43 percent in the United States say that they pass information they have learned from the show to other people.

The socialization value of the dramas becomes clearer now. Their politics-relevant messages are circulated within social networks. We also took note that there was no obvious hesitation in admitting that the information originated from a television drama. About 95 percent of our respondents in Greece and the United States, and 78 percent in the Netherlands, were very comfortable to reveal that they learned the information they were sharing with others from a television drama.

We also asked respondents to specify what they usually discussed about the show. Some mentioned the plot or the action scenes. For example, a Greek viewer of *ER* discussed "the medical cases in the show, how they conduct operations." A Dutch viewer of *The Simpsons* talked about "the jokes, and the good quotes." Others referred to specific information they gained from watching the

Table 5.11 How often do you discuss things that happen in the show?

	Greece %	Netherlands %	U.S. %
Regularly, after every show	29.4	35.3	62.5
Occasionally	63.2	41.2	31.3
Never	7.4	23.5	6.3
Number of responses	68	51	48

shows. For example, a Greek *ER* viewer talked about some methods they used: "It actually looked strange to me that they can cure someone like that." A Greek viewer of *The Simpsons* often engaged in discussions "about political issues and the American way of life."

To provide a more systematic view of the content of our respondents' conversations, we coded their open-ended responses on the basis of several recurring categories: discussions about plot and action, characters and relations, artistic features and format, and information and insights. Our aim was to identify the types of information that run through the viewers' social networks.

We found that viewers in Greece and the United States focus mainly on the plot and the action (69.5 percent and 57 percent, respectively). Characters and relationships, on the other hand, were the strong favorite in the Netherlands (32 percent), where earlier we found increased learning in the relationship category.

As shown in Table 5.12, sharing practical information and insights is less common, but not absent in discussions of the shows. About 8 percent of respondents in Greece and the Netherlands, and 12 percent in the United States mentioned discussion topics that lie outside the purely entertainment-centered topics of conversation.

So, although dramas rarely inspire overt political action, they do motivate many viewers to engage in political discussions. We already noted that entertainment television is seen by many viewers as an occasion for socializing. This is particularly true of Americans who like to discuss the show with others. The answers of our respondents demonstrate the richness of the drama-centered information exchanges in these social networks. We also found that

Table 5.12 What kinds of things do you usually discuss?

	Greece %	Netherlands %	U.S. %
Plot/action	69.5	27.0	57.1
Characters/relations	10.2	32.4	16.7
Information/insights	8.5	8.1	11.9
Other	8.5	32.4	11.9
Artistic features/format	3.4	0	2.4
Number of responses	59	37	42

the lives, experiences, and struggles of the story protagonists in the United States captured the attention and triggered conversational engagement beyond American shores.

As noted earlier, the use of political information is as important for the development of the civic IQ as information acquisition. To examine how viewers use what they learn from the shows, we asked them to link information from the show to hypothetical situations. To see if viewers draw parallels with their own lives, we also asked them to describe how the show resembled or differed from real life, and whether they thought the show is about real people. We then grouped their responses into seven categories: behaviors and reactions; character, personality, and values; habits and lifestyle; problems and worries; weaknesses and virtues; profession and roles; and the catchall category labeled "other." We coded the shows as differing from reality if our subjects characterized them as exaggerated, unrealistic, or idealized.

For example, a Greek viewer of *24* who thought that the characters resembled real people commented, "Yes, when it comes to traitors and terrorists, they are similar because terrorism is a reality." A Greek viewer of *Lost* said, "Of course there are similarities. The island is a small society, and there are vigorous and sensitive people." A Dutch viewer of *Grey's Anatomy* was skeptical: "The plot could be about real people but not about real doctors. The relations are somewhat extreme, but realistic. To me the hospital part is not realistic." A Greek viewer of *CSI* also disagrees: "No, they are not like real people. The characters are idealized." A Greek *ER* viewer, drawing on cultural experiences and indirectly criticizing her own society, noted, "The characters are not the same as Greeks. I don't know about other people, but Greeks are not like this—they are not always doing the right thing."

When viewers compare the characters on the show to real people, they very often find them similar. In fact, about 56 percent of the respondents in Greece and the United States, and 49 percent in the Netherlands consider the characters similar to real people. Interestingly, the Dutch, who are most skeptical about the realism of television dramas, are most likely to point to differences between show characters and real people. The number of viewers who see drama characters as clearly different from regular people stands at

30 percent for the Dutch and drops to 25 percent for Americans and 12.5 percent for Greeks.

When we change the question to ask about the similarities between the show characters and real people, as identified in Table 5.13, notice the intriguing country-based differentiation in responses. Greeks identify more similarities on the basis of character, personality, and values with the characters of the American shows, whereas the Dutch find more similarities in their behaviors and reactions, perhaps reflecting the similarities of the societal context between the United States and the Netherlands. Habits and lifestyle, which are familiar points of reference for the American viewers, seem less realistic in the eyes of Greek viewers, who experience a different everyday reality.

References to drama characters become all the more relevant when people can find parallels in their immediate environment. When we asked our respondents whether they knew people similar to the characters in the show, we received many positive replies. The rate was 60 percent for the Greek sample, but lower for the Dutch (45 percent) and the Americans (36 percent). We conclude that our subjects are adept at assessing and comparing various types of personalities across cultural boundaries. The television dramas helped them in honing these important skills.

To what extent did our respondents draw parallels between their own political reality and the political contexts depicted in the television dramas? To find out, we asked the participants whether

Table 5.13 How are the show people similar to real people?

	Greece %	Netherlands %	U.S. %
Character/personality/values	27.1	20	33.3
Behavior/reactions	18.8	24	29.2
Profession/role	16.7	12	4.2
Problems/worries	10.4	16	12.5
Weaknesses/virtues	6.3	12	4.2
Habits/lifestyle	6.3	12	16.7
Other	14.6	4	0
Number of responses	48	25	24

their favorite television drama presents a realistic picture of life in the United States, and then probed the reasons for their answers. Some found the shows exaggerated or totally unrealistic. Others thought that the political contexts were very specialized or idealized life in the United States.

For example, a Greek viewer of *24* said, "The show exaggerates. I don't believe that it is representative. I think it is somewhat close to reality, but it is not representative." A fellow viewer also found the show unrealistic because "African-Americans are presented as if they are integrated into the society." A Greek viewer of *ER* thought that the show painted a realistic picture of American society as "it touches on it … it doesn't take any position but it presents the situation—i.e., a black doctor has to work harder for recognition." A Dutch *ER* viewer agreed that "There is discrimination. It is realistic." A viewer of *Grey's Anatomy* noted, "The show is realistic. People in the hospital are of different ethnicities. The same applies to the patients. I think that cultural differences are not that big in United States—at least, not as big as they are in the Netherlands." Another Dutch viewer concurred, "I think it is realistic. It does show a picture of the differences between Europeans and Americans. I've been partly raised in America, and I think it's easier to see whether things are true or not."

The aggregate responses in Table 5.14 reveal that about 49 percent of American respondents say that the show presents a realistic picture of life in their country. Amazingly, their score is the highest. Europeans find the dramas substantially less credible. Predictably, Greek participants are more willing than Dutch participants to trust the authenticity of the fictional presentations. Thirty-one percent of Greek respondents consider their drama to be realistic. That compares to 21.6 percent for Dutch viewers, who are more skeptical, most likely because the differentiation between television dramas and actual life is much sharper in the Netherlands.

Sharing Political Insights Across Borders

The ability to accurately compare the political world as reflected in the television drama with your own political reality is a measure of the keenness of the civic IQ. With this in mind, we asked our

Table 5.14 Does the show present a realistic picture of life in the U.S.?

	Greece %	Netherlands %	U.S. %
No	39.1	54.9	34.7
Yes	31.3	21.6	49.0
It depends/to some extent	18.8	15.7	12.2
Not sure	10.9	7.8	4.1
Number of responses	64	51	49

European participants if there were any elements of the show that they would like to emulate in their country. Their responses show whether they use information from the television drama to form their opinions and preferences.

Some viewers mentioned "the infrastructure of this country," as did a Greek viewer of *The Sopranos*. A Dutch viewer of *Grey's Anatomy* would like to borrow from "the education system for doctors—that you will be a paramedic first, and that you go and study from there." A Greek viewer of *ER* noted that in the show, "the health care system is well organized. There is no need to bribe doctors to do their duty." A viewer of *Grey's Anatomy* mentioned, "It would be good to have the fully equipped hospitals and the behavior of medical and paramedical staff." A Dutch viewer of *Lost* touched on values of "altruism and group feeling."

The participants' answers are categorized in Table 5.15. We expected significant differences in the responses of Dutch and Greek respondents, given the socioeconomic and institutional/organizational differences of the two countries.

The Greek responses must be considered in the context of a fragile economy, coupled with anxiety for the future; disaffection with political processes and institutions; and a weak, apathetic, and disengaged civil society (Mouzelis and Pagoulatos, 2002; Demertzis, 1997). The Eurobarometer social climate survey consistently reveals that Greece has one of the lowest levels of life satisfaction in Europe.[4]

Greek viewers were particularly concerned about the functioning of institutions (21.3 percent) and the further development of

Table 5.15 Which elements of the show, absent from your society, would you like to copy?

	Greece %	Netherlands %
Functioning of institutions/services	21.3	10.9
Nothing	19.7	50.0
Technology/infrastructure	19.7	2.2
Values/behaviors	18.0	10.9
Other	8.2	0
Don't know	8.2	26.1
A similar show	4.9	0
Number of responses	61	46

technology and infrastructure (19.7 percent). Eighteen percent wanted improvements in values and behavior.

On the other hand, the Netherlands is among Europe's highest scorers in life satisfaction (Europa report, Eurobarometer 315). Hence, it is not surprising that Dutch viewers exhibit no strong desire for changes in the ways their society functions.

The Greek respondents' far greater skepticism about politics and government emerges equally clearly when asked to rate the trustworthiness of political personalities and institutions. Table 5.16 shows trust ratings for political leaders, the national parliament, the police and the legal system, as well as for the European Parliament and the United Nations. Consistently, Dutch respondents assign significantly higher ratings to all national institutions and the United Nations than their Greek counterparts. However, Greeks and Dutch respondents shared their negative feelings regarding the European Parliament.

Overall, Tables 5.15 and 5.16 show that viewers of television dramas are able to draw parallels between their actual political reality and the examples of institutional, organizational, technological, and other realities depicted in the dramas. They are also able to be critical of the political and social conditions in their native country. Examples of political life in television dramas can color their perceptions and serve as models for change when their own real-life experiences are unsatisfactory.

Table 5.16 Trust in Political Institutions

	Greece	Netherlands
Politicians	4.03[a] (1.77)	6.55[b] (1.10)
Parliament	4.70[a] (1.83)	6.55[b] (1.36)
Legal system	5.42[a] (1.86)	7.40[b] (1.11)
Police	4.87[a] (2.02)	6.94[b] (1.41)
EU Parliament	5.90[a] (1.94)	5.84[a] (1.47)
United Nations	4.25[a] (2.58)	6.17[b] (1.66)
Number of responses	69	51

Next to the mean, the value in parentheses reports standard deviation. Common superscripts (a, b) indicate nonsignificant mean differences at the 0.05 level across rows.

Conclusion

Our analysis shows that the political messages embedded in television dramas can survive the leap across national boundaries. They can promote political learning and enhance the civic IQ among receptive audiences in other countries. The user-friendly dramatic format makes these shows attractive to millions of viewers across the world. Along with the entertainment value comes passive learning.

For the European and U.S. audiences studied here, learning involved mainly the enrichment of existing knowledge, rather than acquisition of new information. This demonstrates that people in different countries who are similar enough in their cultural experiences can process political information that refers to situations beyond their shores.

Information offered by television dramas may be less believable than information offered as news, but it retains informational nourishment nonetheless. In fact, it may actually be more believable when it is embedded in a drama, because nonfictional news from abroad is often distrusted. In addition, passive learning is less likely to arouse skepticism and automatic disbelief than is the case when learning is intentional.

The impact of information from television dramas spreads beyond the confines of the original audience. It tends to circulate within larger communication networks because viewers often discuss the dramas with others. Research on social networks suggests that political engagement increases via discussion in informal social groups, as information is communicated from one individual to another (McClurg, 2003; Huckfeldt, 1979).

The ability of viewers to draw evaluative parallels between situations and characters from the show and real-world social and political conditions is further evidence of learning across borders. There is even evidence of cross-fertilization. Viewers are willing to toy with the idea of adapting and incorporating desirable American practices into their own cultures.

Demonstration of the many shared cultural understandings should not mislead us into believing that differences in political cultures can be ignored. They exist, and they are substantial. The tables in this chapter attest to that fact. Greece and the Netherlands, along with the United States, share many of the fundamentals of culture, such as Western-style democratic traditions, a capitalist-style economy, and religions based on Judeo-Christian beliefs. Nonetheless, their political experiences and settings are different, and these differences are reflected in their reactions to political issues.

CHAPTER SIX
LOOKING BACK AND LOOKING FORWARD

We have come a long way. Before sketching out a possible future where an ample flow of essential information keeps citizens adequately informed, it seems appropriate to review the main points established thus far.

What We Have Learned

Chapter One highlighted the serious disjuncture in democratic theory between claims that public opinion is the bedrock of democracy and charges that most citizens are ignorant about important political facts and issues. If most Americans know little about their government and care even less, as also argued, the notion that our government should and does reflect public opinions is a sham.

The dilemma fades when we differentiate between individual and collective opinions, as political scientists Benjamin Page and Robert Shapiro did in their 1992 landmark study, *The Rational Public: Fifty Years of Trends in Americans' Policy Preferences.* Public opinion—the aggregate that emerges when individual opinions are pooled—is sound, even when individual opinions fall short.

Chapter One also explained that the criteria used in measuring people's knowledge about politics are unscientific because they ignore how human brains actually process information. To make matters worse, poll questions often are ill suited for testing citizens' civic IQ because they call for information that is unrelated to the tasks of citizenship. The questions test individuals' recall of specific facts, rather than their understanding of the meaning and implications derived from these facts.

Measured by realistic criteria, the collective civic IQ seems to be sufficiently astute. The American public understands what is going on in the political environment. This claim about the soundness of public opinion was supported by evidence from public-opinion polls in seven public-policy areas. That evidence confirmed that the public, collectively, pays attention to reports about important political issues. When political situations change markedly, the balance of opinion shifts in ways that are rationally defensible.

Arguments about the soundness of public opinion are often buttressed by accusations that the news media do not supply sufficient information for people to be adequately informed about politics so that they can perform their civic duties well enough. Chapter Two tackled that argument from an exceptionally broad perspective. Rather than analyzing the adequacy of any particular medium, we examined how well media, collectively, cover the range of issues in need of citizen surveillance. Again, the findings aggregated from newspapers, television, cable broadcasts, and blogs are encouraging. Collectively, news media report about a broad range of important public issues.

Chapter Two also added yet another piece to the puzzle of why Americans score so poorly when faced with social scientists' knowledge-test questions. The chapter revealed that poll questions frequently do not correspond to information that was actually available in the news media. It provided examples where knowledge-test questions called for data that had not been aired recently, if ever, in news stories. Framing correct answers for many of the questions was especially difficult because it required ill-defined, complex calculations that went beyond most people's mathematical skills.

Chapter Three voiced concerns that prospects for a sound civic IQ may be dimming because attention to news stories has been declining, while the need for an informed public remains as great as ever. We wondered whether citizenship competency is sliding downhill. How can and do people who slight news stories retain an understanding of their political world? If newspaper reading and attention to news broadcasts are waning in popularity, are there alternative sources of news that can capture mass attention?

Our concerns prompted us to search for political news beyond regular news media. It led us to investigate political content in popular television serial dramas that regularly attract millions of viewers. Many of these dramas are cast into contemporary political scenarios that include controversial political issues. Research demonstrates that dramatic stories, especially when told audiovisually, present excellent, engaging learning situations that attract huge, loyal audiences. Could dramas with story lines that mirror contemporary society be alternate venues for informing people about current politics?

Chapter Three explained how we analyzed the content presented in the television dramas to assess what kind of realistic and reasonably accurate political information they provided. But do viewers of these dramas actually pay attention to the political issues raised in the dramas? Do they trust the accuracy of the political information, and do they learn from it? Chapter Three described how we found answers to these questions through exceptionally open, unconventional interviews, which were designed to avoid some common interview problems.

The insights that we gained from our interviews with American fans of our sample of serial dramas are covered in Chapter Four. The chapter outlines the stories that our interviewees watched. It records typical politically relevant observations, as well as comments that emerged from the interviews and from message boards linked to the shows.

Chapter Four demonstrated the power of dramas to transport viewers' minds to far-from-home locations, where they savor familiar and unfamiliar experiences. For instance, viewers might vicariously experience being inside the White House and watching the president, or they might observe a busy emergency room and watch how the doctors and nurses do their jobs.

The chapter also reported our viewers' own, unprompted analyses of how they reacted to the story lines, and used the vicarious drama experiences to form impressions and to assess the accuracy of the information. Their comments provide priceless insights into the diversity of impressions, feelings, and thoughts that dramas can generate. Still, what viewers reported during the interviews is obviously an incomplete summation. They did not tell us everything that they might have said. Yet, it was enough to confirm our expectations that millions of people, even when they avoid news broadcasts, get current political information through entertainment channels.

Chapter Five demonstrated that what people learn is structured in part by their cultural background. The chapter tabulated the answers to each interview question. It included the U.S. data, but the main focus was on data from the Netherlands and Greece. The differences in Europeans' reactions to the drama stimuli are significant, but they are not vast. The findings confirm the observation made by political scientists Michael Delli Carpini and Bruce Williams that "Politics is built on deep-seated cultural values and beliefs that are embedded in the seemingly nonpolitical aspects of public and private life" (Delli Carpini and Williams, 2001, p. 161).

The interviews in the Netherlands and Greece also show that people's experiences in different cultures can be similar enough so that they can relate to the same shows. People in non-Western cultures would have a bit more trouble relating, but not much. The fact that the dramas are successfully syndicated in Asia and the Middle East is strong evidence of their cross-cultural appeal.

Why the Findings Matter

For researchers of public opinion and political communication, this book provides examples of alternative routes to learning about politics. It demonstrates the importance of television serial dramas in building and maintaining the civic IQ. This vastly popular form of entertainment does indeed offer a modest, but by no means trivial, diet of political information that enhances understanding of politics.

Drama contributions are particularly useful to the many citizens who learn more easily from pictures and sounds than from words.

In fact, visually oriented audience members may gain as much or more useful information from the visual fare in dramas as verbally oriented audience members gain from verbal texts (Prior, 2004). However, the substance of what they learn may not be the same.

On Media also shows that political learning covers diverse aspects of politics drawn from many policy realms. This has clear implications for gauging and theorizing about the type of information that is essential for sustaining the civic IQ. The research clearly demonstrates that knowledge tests that call for recall of specific verbal descriptions do not do justice to the many citizens who understand the complexity of the political world without recalling proper names, designations, or numerical data.

Our findings are also important for public policies. Because citizens do learn from entertainment shows, public organizations and governments can use television dramas to educate them about political issues that would otherwise escape their attention. Chapter Five confirms that such messages travel well even across borders. In the United States, drama shows have educated the public about problems like violence against women, HIV/AIDS, alcohol abuse, and environmental protection.

The American movie industry has worked closely with relevant public agencies, generating tip sheets for television writers and producers, organizing expert panel discussions to examine the implications of dramatizing information, and conducting research on audience needs and effects. Public-policy issues raised in television dramas can lead to changes in political attitudes and actions.

Our study highlights the significance of discussions about the content of shows. In Greece, the Netherlands, and particularly the United States, television dramas often spur conversations about political issues. These discussions spread through conversation networks and bring average citizens together in a way that news broadcasts largely fail to do. Besides producing better-informed citizens, talking about television dramas in informal social settings can create social capital.

Finally, our research demonstrates that the systematic examination of how citizens understand politics via entertainment offerings is a promising field of study. It can uncover the complexities of political learning and the ways in which popular entertainment fare succeeds in shaping how citizens see and experience their political world. Political scientists have only recently ventured into this important research area.

What Is Learning and How Should We Measure It?

In this chapter, we further dissect the learning process, based on findings from the interviews. More nuanced analysis reveals that the scope of learning from television dramas is far broader than what cruder measures have been able to detect.

Multiple Facets of the Learning Process

The largely open-ended conversations during the interviews taught us that analyzing *learning* about politics involves far more than testing how well or poorly subjects remember selected portions of recorded stimulus information. It also involves:

- Appraising gradations in the amounts of learning
- Assessing the types of information most likely to be learned
- Distinguishing between learning of facts and comprehending of relationships that are involved in human interactions
- Measuring respondents' ability and inclination to form and express evaluations of situations
- Gauging respondents' ability to link new information to prior experiences

Such detailed scrutiny of learning requires complex calculations. It is worth the effort because it provides sharper tools for gauging to what extent information stimuli actually convey political information that enhances the civic IQ.

Let's begin with a specific example. Your best friend's sister, Susan, has just finished her first year of high school. You ask Susan what she has learned in her civics class. "Oh," she says, "we talked a lot about current problems like dealing with uninsured patients in hospitals, or whether children should be returned to parents who are recovering alcoholics, or what the president should do when Congress doesn't cooperate."

How would you react? Shocked that this did not sound like *regular* course material that high schools *ought to teach*? Or pleased that Susan's civics class had stimulated her to ponder vexing public problems, albeit in somewhat cursory and disorganized fashion? How do you and should you, as a citizen and possibly a parent, define *real learning*? The answer to that question has been hotly disputed among professional educators, political analysts, and members of the public.

Opinion cleavages about the nature of learning reflect disagreements about the goals that it should achieve. People vary in their expectations about the general knowledge of a given subject area that the proverbial everyone should have in the best of all worlds, as well as the knowledge they absolutely must have in the real world. Such disagreements are common. People rarely agree even about the knowledge that professionals like doctors, lawyers, and science teachers should have to earn a license for performing their tasks competently.

My goal in this book is clear. I sought to evaluate whether twenty-first century Americans know and understand enough about politics to adequately perform citizenship duties in a complex democratic society. When we measured the extent of political learning from an information source, we were looking for knowledge and understanding gains that relate to the individual and collective civic IQ.

Composing Relevant Interview Questions

Interview questions that probe for political learning and analysis of the answers must vary depending on the dimensions of human knowledge that the investigator wants to gauge. For research about the scope of political knowledge that monitorial citizens need, our interviews and subsequent analysis needed to focus on indicators that would show whether our respondents had gained any lasting insights into politics that were likely to help them in performing their citizenship duties:

- Did their responses show that they could grasp the implications of politically relevant information and that they could integrate it into their existing fund of political knowledge?
- Could they project consequences by inferring general concepts from particular situations?
- Could they make sense of stories, even when the happenings in the serial dramas were not actually shown on screen but were merely implied, talked about, or started but not completed (Franklin, 2006)? Were they able to fill in the blanks?

The questions needed to be open-ended enough so that viewers could enrich the images offered on the screen with information that they already held in memory. We anticipated that viewers who were totally unfamiliar with the kinds of situations presented on the screen would characterize them as incomprehensible and something to which they could not relate. They would also be more likely to misinterpret the scenarios.

Pieces of political information—in dramas or news—are stimuli. If they resonate with viewers' experiences, viewers provide much of the content that gives meaning to the stimuli. If a story does not resonate with the viewers' past learning or major interests, it is likely to be ignored.

The Abundance of Response Choices

In our appraisal of learning, we did not expect that viewers exposed to the same episodes of a drama would draw parallel meanings from them. The end results and consequences of making sense of new messages are rarely uniform. Analyses of jury deliberations in criminal cases demonstrate this point very clearly (Loftus, 1996). Precisely how viewers integrate testimony into their existing funds of knowledge depends on their particular memories and on their learning styles. That is why prospective jurors are screened to determine whether their values and beliefs potentially prejudice their verdicts.

Our interviews for the current study, as well as empirical analyses of learning in specific real-world political contexts, make it clear that basic orientations, values, and prior beliefs substantially constrain the influence of new information stimuli (Gilardi, 2010). Moreover, it matters how vivid and emotional the images and opinions are that individuals hold in their memories. In general, people are keener to incorporate new evidence into their beliefs if the change does not entail sharp departures from their prior orientations.

Audiences of a particular show or news program usually can agree about the meanings that the messages are intended to convey. That happens because producers of these programs use standard audiovisual lingo so that audiences coming from different backgrounds can comprehend the story line. Showing a crowd of emaciated people in front of a food store signifies poverty nearly everywhere, while vistas of well-kept mansions in pristine neighborhoods tell the opposite story.

Audiences understand the sound and symbol combinations that have become customary over time for conveying specific ideas. Moreover, in the case of television serial dramas, the characters have become familiar to viewers over extended periods of time. That makes it much easier to assign multifaceted meanings to what they are saying and doing. While viewers usually agree about what happened in a particular episode, they frequently disagree about the implications of the situation and about the characters' (or producer's) motivations.

In addition to the obviously intended meanings that stories convey to audiences, individual audience members may also extract unique personal meanings. These personal meanings often emerged in the interviews. Respondents would recount the connotative meanings conveyed in shows or newscasts, and then meld them with their personal memories and the facts of their current personal lives.

The Choice Process

Figure 6.1 identifies the three major information streams that audience members must integrate:

- New information that is reaching them and requires processing
- The information selectively extracted from their memories
- The information impinging on them from their environments at the time of exposure

The Mood and Setting designation, at the top of the diagram, refers to the collective and individual emotional and judgmental reactions that environments elicit. Judging by their conversations, our respondents were fully aware that learning is a multidimensional, context-dependent activity.

Mr. Webster Concurs

Webster's Dictionary confirms this broad conception of *learning* when it defines the process as gaining new knowledge, understanding, or skills, and as the ability to modify existing knowledge and use it appropriately (*Webster's Third New International Dictionary*, 1966). The dictionary attributes learning to three types of activities: study, instruction, or experience. It notes that learning may entail conscious effort, or it may occur effortlessly without the

Figure 6.1 The Information Streams That Audiences Must Integrate

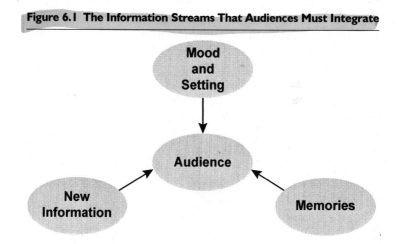

learner's intention or even awareness. Subject-wise, it may involve learning something totally unknown before, or it may involve learning much more, or a tad more, about something previously known.

The discussion that follows puts some more empirical meat on Webster's definition skeleton. In prior chapters, we have discussed the kinds of knowledge, understanding, and skills that our respondents and the people who posted web messages learned from the dramas. Precisely, how had their knowledge and understanding changed as a consequence of watching the dramas? How was their existing knowledge modified by information from the dramas, as described by them in the recorded interviews and as judged by us, based on their comments?

Seven Learning Categories

Our interviews disclosed seven different kinds of learning. They ranged from learning major or minor facts to comprehending the interplay of various political factors and to drawing fresh conclusions based on new observations. As Table 5.8 in Chapter Five illustrates, these are important gradations that are essential for understanding the impact of new messages on existing knowledge. Yet, most research about learning has largely ignored these nuances, focusing exclusively on learning major new facts (Alexander et al., 2009; Murphy and Mason, 2006). Consequently, the extent of learning about politics has been vastly underestimated.

In real-life situations, people's knowledge tends to be more highly rated if it is coupled with experiences pertaining to that knowledge. The same should hold true for the vicarious experiences that people encounter in television dramas that deepen and broaden their knowledge. Unfortunately, that does not happen. People are rarely given any credit at all for their vicarious experiences, which they may savor more accurately than when they are embroiled in real-life situations.

Table 6.1 shows the seven common types of learning listed in Table 5.8, along with indications of how frequently each category of learning appears in our recorded interviews:

- "Add major facts" means gaining important new insights about politics.
- "Add minor facts" means fleshing out existing politically relevant knowledge.
- The "new slants" categories mean viewing political facts or relationships from previously ignored perspectives. As one viewer put it, "I never thought about it in that way." New slants may also involve a deepening of existing knowledge, as noted by the viewer who said emphatically, "I knew pollution was bad, but not that bad!"
- "Add vicarious experiences" refers to when respondents talked about the unique impact that sprang from actually observing relationships in action, rather than merely hearing about them.
- "Add evaluations" identifies expressions of newly formed opinions about previously known situations.
- "Refresh fading memories" refers to statements that viewing drama episodes had refreshed the respondent's memories about forgotten situations. For example, several *Lost* viewers commented that setting up a new government on a deserted island reminded them of similar situations in William Golding's famous novel *Lord of the Flies*. Chances are that they had not retrieved details from the novel for many years. Recalling these details may have sharpened them in their memories and possibly brought previously neglected aspects into focus (Schreiber, 2007; Specio and Adolphs, 2007).

Learning was rated as follows:

- Often means it was evident in 50 percent or more of the interviews.
- Some means that the particular level of learning was detected in 11 to 49 percent of the interviews.
- Rarely means that 10 percent or fewer of the interviews featured the particular level of learning.

The mental exercise involved in searching for relevant memories and comparing past experiences with new ones may not always

Table 6.1 The Prevalence of Various Types of Learning

Learning	Often 50%+	Some 11–49%	Rarely 0–10%
Add major facts		X	
Add minor facts	X		
New slants on facts		X	
New slants on relationships	X		
Add vicarious experiences	X		
Add evaluations		X	
Refresh fading memories			X

constitute *learning*. The interviews do not make it entirely clear whether and when memory searches and comparisons add anything lasting to a viewer's fund of knowledge, beyond reviving what that viewer already knew. For example, studies of the impact of *The West Wing* claim that the show primes viewers' thinking about real presidents (Holbert et al., 2003; Gans-Boriskin and Tisinger, 2005). But do the primes measurably increase the viewers' fund of knowledge about the presidency? The answer remains moot.

Frequency Variations

Table 6.1 clearly shows that enrichment of existing information was far more prevalent than learning major new facts. It also shows that vicarious political experiences were common. According to the interviews, that was true especially when episodes demonstrated how people interact in complex situations.

New perspectives and new evaluations of existing knowledge were less usual. Learning truly major new facts was comparatively rare. That makes sense when you consider that most of the learning from these shows was passive (Baum, 2005). Major learning usually entails conscious effort.

Some interviewees, as well as posters to message boards, even expressed resentment about the inclusion of political lessons in their drama shows, especially when they suspected that these lessons were intentional. Here's a typical post, selected from literally hundreds of similar ones: "I am sick of that Africa thing. If I wanted to watch Darfur, I'll turn in to CNN or the evening news. The show's name is ER, not Adventures in Africa."

Missing Elements

Table 6.1 records only whether certain types of learning took place and how commonly they occurred. The table does not deal with the specific subject matter that was learned, the correctness of the information, or its importance for the performance of civic duties.

Our research design forecloses gauging the full range of information that our interviewees or web posters learned. We cannot accurately assess their prior knowledge, even to the limited extent possible in some laboratory experiments. Nor did we test completely everything that our respondents may have learned about issues to which they alluded. We merely sampled it, and therefore understate the full scope of learning. We also do not know which types of episodes are never or rarely remembered, or how many different types of frames were in each viewer's repertoire.

However, the demographic data that we gathered at the end of the interviews support a well-known phenomenon that is as true in learning from dramas as it is in learning from regular news: People who already know a lot ordinarily learn more than people who know little. Information-rich individuals have a broader store of memories available to provide the hooks needed for capturing the sense of new messages.

We also know that the shows that are richest in political information tend to attract the most educated and media-savvy audiences, because they can relate more easily to the content of the drama (Fitzgerald, 2005). In our viewer sample, people who are averse to politics were unlikely to be fans of *The West Wing*. But, given the pervasiveness of political content in television serial dramas, this does not mean that they escaped political contexts or shut them out when watching episodes.

Interview Examples

Table 6.2 presents comments excerpted from the recorded interviews that demonstrate what sorts of things viewers learned and in what manner. The table also displays two elusive aspects of learning that were excluded from Table 6.1 because respondents rarely spoke about them. Nonetheless, these processes most likely played an important role when respondents had watched the show and had become engrossed in the story:

- "Sharper thinking" refers to the fact that the vicarious experiences created by the dramas, just like real-life experiences, heighten the viewers' reactions to the stimuli and to their associated memories.
- "Insights into thinking processes" covers comments that people made about their thinking habits. These commentaries about how the respondent formulated an opinion or evaluation usually surfaced in the interviews during follow-up queries that asked "Why are you saying this?" Our interview recordings reveal much greater awareness of reasoning processes than we had anticipated.

The reasons for "sharper thinking" are readily explained by human physiology. When the past comes to life again, many people become emotionally aroused. Their mental functions are sharpened because their bodies secrete hormones that make them more alert. Elements that were previously slighted may come into fuller focus. The arousal, which neuroscientists can now document with functional magnetic resonance imaging (fMRI) technologies, makes learning more encompassing and profound, so that people notice and remember more details. It is like focusing a camera lens so that a somewhat blurred image becomes sharper.

The comments in Table 6.2 originate from a very rich menu of remarks about a wealth of important issues. They show that people go beyond absorbing new information. They evaluate it in terms of its merits and its significance for various situations, including their own welfare.

Table 6.2 Learning Category Examples from Interviews

Learning Categories	Viewer Comments
Add major facts	[I learned about] U.S. policy on negotiating with terrorists; how FBI and counterterrorism units work; how a school voucher system works; [the show] broadens your knowledge. There are conditions that exist you never thought of before
Add minor facts	I learned about the date rape drug Ecstasy; [I learned about] tools and techniques used in crime detection; how to survive a bomb explosion; lifestyles of gay people
New slants on facts	[I learned about] how individual actions can have international consequences like when one person kills a Chinese embassy member; how fear of malpractice suits keep doctors from admitting mistakes; [the show] has changed my perception of politics
New slants on relationships	[It shows] how tensions develop between police and actual crime scene investigators or lawyers; [I think that] you can get things out of watching how others interact and respond to things; some of the interactions on the show [Lost] tell you a lot about why people fight and why people get along ... how people from different cultures act
Add experiential insights	Seeing how politics really works—like how the president and Congress work together—deepens understanding of politics; [ER shows you] unequal treatment options between poor and rich; The West Wing teaches you about decision-making, negotiation, consultation at the cabinet level; when a likable key guy whom you see every week gets stabbed, that's memorable
Add evaluations	I never knew how difficult it was for public institutions to cope with uninsured patients; I wouldn't say that I condemn it [torturing terrorism suspects], but I don't support it; I actually thought about what [presidential action] I would support; I would never do that
Refresh fading memories	It refreshes my memory ... sometimes it gets me to check out things I've read before; episodes remind me of real-life counterparts; the spill at the nuclear power plant reminds me about the accident that actually happened; that spoof about Enron [The Simpsons] brought it all back to me—my friend didn't get it

Table 6.2 (continued)

Learning Categories	Viewer Comments
Sharper thinking	It has made me more aware ... more observant; the show has increased my interest in politics; when I discuss the show, things get clearer ... we talk about foreign policy, minimum wage; we talk about how the show correlates with our own political situation; when I hear about how effective AA programs are, I wonder about my Dad dying from alcoholism
Insights into thinking processes	I take my experiences and bring them to the show, and use the information from the show to broaden my perspective; I try to change my views a little based on how they portray an issue

The comments also document that people dwell on interpersonal relationships in public and personal situations. In fact, neuroscience research shows that the human brain has a mirror neuron system that actually reenacts situations that people are witnessing on the screen. Mirror neurons allow humans to mentally place themselves into the roles of others, and envision how they would feel and act if they were walking in those shoes (Keysers, 2010).

Finally, the refresh fading memories category illustrates the close link between fact and fiction when fictional events evoke recall of prior real-life experiences.

Like several other tables in this book, Table 6.2 demonstrates that average people do think about politically important issues. Nonetheless, even if Table 6.2 displayed all of the recorded comments of our respondents, it would by no means cover all that citizens need to know collectively to provide solid bases for political decisions.

If we had interviewed a much larger sample of respondents, the picture would improve substantially, but it would undoubtedly still fall far short of the ideal. The reason is simple. The notion that citizens, collectively, can know about everything that is of major political importance is an unrealizable dream. It is blind to the complexities of human environments, the limitations of human-learning capacities, and the shortcomings of human motivations.

Ascertaining the Sources of Learned Information

How do we know that people learned the information reported during our interviews from the shows, rather than from other sources? We have numerous indicators, though none provide absolute proof.

I already mentioned that participants in the initial experiments confirmed that specific knowledge had originated with the show and used language borrowed from *The Sopranos* clips during focus group sessions. In addition, many interviewees said that they discussed the show during broadcasts and afterward with fellow watchers, friends, family, and coworkers. These discussions rehearsed the scenes that had been viewed and engraved them more deeply in memory. They also enriched the array of perspectives that emerged from dramas.

Another sign that information reported in interviews came from the shows is the fact that all viewers could report the general thrust of episodes that they had recently watched, and they described details that could have come only from watching their show. Viewers often reported experiencing situations similar to those in the drama they had watched, and expressed opinions, judgments, and evaluations drawing on their own experiences as well as the show. For instance, one *ER* viewer noted, "You can compare someone's story to your own life," and then proceeded to link events in the show to her volunteer health services on behalf of the poor and her own antiwar activities.

Viewers also draw parallels between characters and situations in the dramas and real-life people and events. In fact, musings about who in the fictional situation resembles which real-life person in appearance and behavior are very common. Similarly, people like to compare situations because it helps them in making sense of what is happening. The severity of the economic depression of the 1970s that forms the background of *That 70's Show* becomes starkly evident when viewers can compare it to their own experiences in times of economic hardship.

Viewers also commented on the thrust of political perspectives featured in various shows, such as the idealistic portrayal of *The West Wing* president and far more sinister characterization of the *24* presidential incumbent. Real-life situations then became the foil for comparing and judging the fictional events.

Comparing situations, drawing parallels, and making judgments about the merits of situations and people all are mental activities that may modify existing knowledge and become *learning*. Table 6.1 showed that half or more of our respondents learned by developing new slants on relationships. These new appraisals often sprang from comparing different people and different events and trying to evaluate them. Similarly, the new slants on facts and new evaluations that 11 to 49 percent of our respondents developed often sprang from comparisons or efforts to evaluate situations.

Viewer immersion in the drama was also clear from the many reports about emotional reactions. Phrases like "It really bothers me," "I am upset," "I cried when that happened," and "It gave me nightmares" are sprinkled throughout the interviews. Some viewers even reported screaming at their television set to stop the progress of events that were harming their favorite characters. Most people have cried or laughed when watching a movie or television show, or have seen others who, at least temporarily, are deeply touched by this make-believe world. Their minds have left the reality around them, so that they are actually experiencing an alternative world (Stromberg, 2009).

As previously mentioned, we also know that emotional arousal heightens the impact of information and makes it more memorable. But we still lack solid evidence to prove beyond a doubt that emotional arousal leads to greater clarity of insights. Some evidence indicates that, at times, it may actually obstruct clear thinking (North and Pfefferbaum, 2002).

The belief that the information that our interviewees gave us did indeed come from the dramas is also buttressed by their claims that they often checked drama data against real-world data to confirm or refute the accuracy of information. For example, several viewers told us that they had checked the accuracy of reports about torturing prisoners or conditions in refugee camps, or denial of medical services to the indigent.

A few viewers speculated about hidden meanings and hidden purposes that producers of the show might have, such as advocating specific environmental policies or laws to safeguard the civil rights of gay people. As mentioned in Chapter Four, some thought that shows might be a trial balloon for testing the public's reaction to prospective governmental actions. When viewers suspected ulterior motives for the shows' plots, they watched episodes closely for possible cues. They often complained about feeling manipulated.

Adapting the News to the Changing News Environment

Unlike dramas that hold the attention of their regular audiences year after year, most current newspaper and news broadcasts seem no longer able to attract many members of their former mass audiences, especially those in younger age groups. Could that trend be reversed for audiences who prefer news in nonfictional formats? We now turn to that issue, coming full circle from discussing nonfictional news in the opening chapters, to dissecting political information in fictional form in Chapters Three through Five, to suggesting reforms for nonfictional formats in this chapter.

Attention-Arousal Factors

Attention arousal is the most important aspect of attracting and keeping audiences, and giving them chances to learn. I began to investigate the attention-arousal puzzle after encountering unexplained variations in attention to television news stories.

Some news stories were able to attract more than half of a national audience; others that involved quite similar situations left much of the potential audience unengaged (Neuman et al., 2007). What accounts for the difference? Is there a threshold that attention triggers must cross to turn noteworthy stories consumed by a fraction of the national audience into news that engages majorities?

Answers to such questions are crucial when we contemplate changes in news offerings that might slow or even reverse audience shrinkages that threaten the soundness of the civic IQ. Analysts and news providers need to know which combinations of stimuli garner and retain the largest audiences for political news, at a time when competition for audiences has become keener than ever before thanks to the Internet.

My research on attention arousal targeted factors that were most likely to attract mass audiences to particular news events (Graber, 2007). I focused on the content and presentation style of real-life stories that had attracted "a great deal" of attention from more than half of the national audience sampled in monthly polls conducted by the Pew Research Center for the People & the Press. Each of these stories could be matched with news reports involving very similar situations that had proven far less captivating. In Pew's news-interest surveys, respondents are asked periodically whether they have followed selected important news stories very closely, fairly closely, not too closely, or not at all closely.

For example, the news media gave extensive, multiday coverage to two space-shuttle explosions: the Challenger spacecraft in 1986 and the Columbia shuttle seven years later. Seven astronauts were killed in each incident. Of the respondents in Pew's national sample, 80 percent said that they had followed the Challenger story very closely when questioned shortly after the incident. The corresponding figure for the Columbia story was 46 percent. What accounts for the large difference?

To find out, we analyzed seven arrays of stories with disparate audience attention scores. They included shootings at public elementary and high schools that killed young students, racial incidents that provoked urban riots in the United States, and U.S. military interventions abroad. We scored all stories on 21 separate features that had been identified in the scholarly literature as reasons for attracting large audiences for a story. Table 6.3 presents these elements.

Of the 21 elements, 11 elements related to the substance of each news story, such as the kinds of people involved in the situation, the nature of the frames used to tell the story, and the vividness

Table 6.3 Attention-Arousal Elements

Categories	Elements
Dramatic Content	Dramatic facts: Severity of actual or potential harm; number of affected people
	Open conflict among political elites
	Dramatic audiovisuals
	Dramatic sounds
	Major violations of social norms
	Numbers of appealing characters, e.g., children, seniors, friendly military
	Numbers of scary characters
	Numbers of reassuring characters
	Numbers of human interest frames
	Numbers of conflict frames
	Numbers of powerless frames
Presentation Features	Length of coverage time
	Numbers of stories
	Numbers of coverage days
	Numbers of action scenes
	Numbers of first section placements
	Numbers of close-up views and nearby sounds
Contextual Matters	Numbers of supporting surrounding stories
	Numbers of arousing links to collective memories
	Numbers of important distracting elements
	Major weaknesses in competing story in content or presentation

of its audiovisual casting. Six of the elements concerned presentation issues, such as the number of close-ups, the length of stories, and the nature and frequency of follow-up stories. Four elements involved contextual matters, like the substance of other stories in the same broadcast and the political climate at the time.

The most important conclusion from the study was that emotion-arousing features that were pictured or suggested were the strongest inducements to lure large numbers of audience members to pay close attention to political news. The finding held true for all stories, irrespective of their topic (Graber, 2007).

Stories that lacked in stirring elements riveted the attention of less than half of the audience, and in most cases, far less. It was equally important that all of the top attention-getters featured multiple arousing elements in various combinations. It seems that, on average, stories become powerful magnets for a majority of viewers only if they excel in at least 13 of the 21 elements we measured. The mix varied, but fear factors were always present. While violence was a common stimulant, nonviolence prevailed overall.

All of the top attention-getting stories featured an assortment of the kinds of threats and uncertainties that bedevil human lives but do not usually involve physical violence. The apparent need for multiple rousing stimuli suggests either that it takes a combination of arousal factors to break across individual attention thresholds or that stories loaded with arousing elements attract larger audiences because they provide a broader array of lures for people with different tastes.

The fact that nearly all of the high-attention stories involved dramatic situations is in line with neuroscience findings that emotional arousal alerts people's senses and captures their interest (Gazzaniga, 1992, 1998; Damasio, 1994, 1999, 2003; Goleman, 1995). Neuroscience research also confirms the findings in this book and other studies that information about dangers lurking in people's environment need not come from personal involvements. Experiencing alarming situations vicariously, through factual or fictional stories, is sufficient to spur attention (Bradley, 2004; Bradley et al., 2001; MacKuen et al., 2001).

Core emotions—like hatred, anxiety, fear, and high elation—are especially potent in stimulating people to pay close attention and to retain details of the situation in long-term memory. By contrast, when arousal stimuli are weak, they are less likely to be noticed, less likely to be remembered, and less stirring when people do take notice.

The length of coverage time was another significant factor in attention arousal in the stories that we analyzed. Stories attracted large audiences if they were substantially longer in minutes of television coverage on a single day or on successive days than their less-noticed sister stories. Lengthier coverage allowed for ampler presentation of high-stimulus factors and for repetitions of the most disturbing pictures.

Dramatizing the News

There is no reason why the features that excite audiences and make them watch stories cannot be adapted for regular news programs that deal with situations that monitorial citizens should know. This book brims with evidence that serious political issues can be couched into dramatic formats, and that people learn far more from messages presented in such formats than from the usual dispassionate, purely factual news accounts. When stories do not merely describe happenings, but instead enact real situations embedded in meaningful contexts, viewers feel and react like witnesses at the scene. Their hearts and minds move into the realities that their eyes and ears are watching and hearing (Stromberg, 2009).

If major American news venues patterned their political news broadcasts more along the lines that make entertainment shows so attractive for huge, heterogeneous audiences, the end result could be a more engaged citizenry who feel they are part of the political "show," rather than distant observers watching an obscure charade. Walter Cronkite pioneered this type of reporting in his legendary *You Are There* broadcasts, beginning in the late 1950s. The popular series, which he hosted, re-created historical events by reporting them as if they were breaking news stories. People became involved in these long-gone historical events because they felt like participants. Most current news story formats lack that dramatic quality.

In fact, formats that focus on unadorned facts and figures often arouse negative reactions because of the prevalence of *data phobia.* Like the better-known *math phobia,* it means that a lot of people dislike information studded with precise numbers and names. They find it boring. If they process it at all, they are likely to exclude it from long-term memory (Graber, 2001).

Boring formats are the Achilles' heel of current news offerings. They explain why people have become *news grazers.* On average, they visit five to six news sites, but generally spend only about 3 minutes in total—roughly 30 seconds per site—on skimming the information (Pew Research Center, 2010b).

Reshaping Storytelling

Several other factors should be considered in news-reshaping efforts. The time allotted to most current news stories is one of them. It is too short.

Most news reports do not allow sufficient time to encase the story in essential background information, and they are short on memory-enhancing repetitions. Whenever audiences become interested in a topic, they are willing and eager to watch it develop at some length. The behavior of serial drama audiences is just one of many examples.

Drama viewers' reactions show that audiences enjoy it when basic news themes are repeated. They can watch their favorite character make the same kinds of mistakes time and time again. Continuity of themes is common in regular newscasts as well. They dwell on recurring events like the ups and downs of the economy, scandalous behaviors by public figures, and the successes and failures of the business community. But the cyclical nature of problems becomes less clear in news stories than in dramas, because the names of the characters and locations change, and reporters rarely highlight how ordinary major problems really are. Doing so would make it easier for audiences to fill in the many blanks generally left by news reports.

Unlike the style of regular news, the political dialogue in television dramas is down-to-earth and often funny. Episodes are told in ordinary language and stress the human complexities that are inevitable when flesh-and-blood people are involved. Compared to news stories that routinely feature multiple interpretations of the same facts to satisfy "objectivity" norms, drama episodes usually present clear causal chains, so that villains and heroes are readily identifiable (Jones, 2005).

Giving stories a clear focus makes them less confusing and allows people to relate to them more easily. This does not mean that stories must ignore challenges to the favored views. It does mean that they should take a clear stand that tells audiences which perspectives are preferable and why. Audiences can then accept or reject the position.

Tailoring News to Varied Tastes

Modern technology has spawned a large crop of new information providers who broadcast news throughout the day and night. To serve monitorial citizens who differ in ideology, age, ethnicity, and many other significant respects, it is essential that information providers tailor their offerings to the needs and wants of specific audience types. It is especially important to provide news that interests young Americans who need to understand the political currents that are shaping the future of their political world (Christensen and Haas, 2005).

As Michael Ignatieff wrote in 1984, "We need language adequate to the times we live in. We need to see how we live now and we can only see with words and images which leave us no escape into nostalgia for some other time and place" (Ignatieff, p. 141).

Concerns that news diversification is unprofitable are unfounded according to a study by the Project for Excellence in Journalism (Rosenstiel et al., 2000). Because there are two major types of audiences for political news—lovers of soft human-interest news and lovers of more serious hard news—either format can attract and hold mass audiences and yield adequate profits for television stations (Gottlieb and Pertilla, 2001). Given the multichannel capacity of high-definition television (HDTV), television stations can easily offer several versions of each type of news in their programs to accommodate the varied tastes of their viewers.

Cable television already offers news designed to appeal to distinct audience segments. FOX News and MSNBC deal with the same body of newsworthy information. But one frames it to please loyal conservative viewers, and the other frames it to lure loyal liberal viewers. Fortunately, each outlet also features some stories from the other side of the ideological fence. You may decry polarization of news broadcasts and audiences, but it is preferable to losing news audiences entirely when they are no longer turned on by more neutral news formats.

Ending on a Positive Note

Producing news that nourishes the civic IQ adequately has always been and will always be a major challenge. But it is not beyond reach, because average Americans still deem information about politics important and want to know about it.

National polls show that only 14 percent of the American public is totally disinterested in political information and does not seek it out, although each day, half of the disinterested encounter it inadvertently (Pew Research Center, 2008b). The remaining 86 percent keep in touch with the political scene, using a blend of online and traditional print and television sources, and, of course, entertainment shows that are suffused with politically relevant information (Pew Research Center, 2010b).

Entertainment shows contribute significantly to the nation's political health because they stimulate thinking about political matters that keeps interest in politics alive. Television serial dramas play a unique role as part of the nation's politically relevant entertainment. Unlike the talking-head shows that concentrate on mocking politicians and their policies, and making politics seem like a game of scoundrels, the dramas create lifelike political experiences. Episodes transform a sizable portion of viewers from being political spectators to becoming vicarious participants in the realities of political life. Although their immersion in politics is fleeting and mostly shallow, its impact is cumulative and becomes measurable over time. And therein lies the potency of the dramas analyzed in this book.

It is no small achievement in our distracting and distracted world to transform ordinary Americans, briefly but regularly, into political insiders who glimpse the essence of politics and make sound sense of it.

Appendix A
The Interviewer Protocol

This appendix describes the interview setup, questions, directions, and coding suggestions.

Interview Setup

The interviews were set up as follows:

1. Contact potential interview subjects.
2. Introduce yourself as a university researcher who has heard that *x* is a regular viewer of the *yyy* show. Is that correct?
3. Explain that the project seeks to assess what people learn. Findings will be presented at scholarly conferences and in scholarly writings.
4. Assure the potential subject that participants will not be identified. If direct quotes are used, they will be attributed to fake names.
5. May we continue with an about 30-minute interview now and tape it, or will another time be more convenient? If the latter, set up a time.
6. In every third interview, ask if another person in the household who does *not* view this show can be interviewed now or later. If later, get times and contact data.

7. Offer thanks at the end of the interview.

Whenever convenient, ask respondent for names and telephone numbers of potential interviewees for their show or other dramas that are in our project. Leave them a contact number for you if they don't have the telephone numbers at hand.

Questions About Shows Plus Some Coding Suggestions

The following are some questions asked about the show, along with some coding suggestions.

1. Tell me why you like to watch the *yyy* show? What do you get out of it?
   a. Excitement, entertainment
   b. Vicarious enjoyment of experiences of others
   c. Like to see how others dress, furnish apartments, etc.
   d. Artistic features, photography, dialogue, etc.
   e. Learn to handle similar experiences, as in b.
   f. Copy clothing, furnishing, etc.
   g. Other (specify)
2. a.) Do you ever learn anything that you can use in your own life?

   Often; sometimes; rarely; never

   b.) What is it?

   Examples from *ER*: Understand how hectic the emergency room is; expect to wait after arrival; doctors are likely to make mistakes, possibly fatal; ask questions when you think they are making a mistake; call 911 in an emergency rather than the driving patient to the emergency room
3. a.) Does it bother you that the information comes from a fiction show?

   None; some; a lot

   b.) Does it make the information less believable?

   No; some; a lot

4. a.) How often do you talk with others about things happening on this show?

Regularly; after every show; occasionally; never

b.) What kinds of things do you usually discuss?

Examples: Plot of episode; implications; physical appearances; acting quality

5. If the viewer has used the information learned from show, was the outcome satisfactory?

Yes; no; partly

a.) Did you pass the information on to others?

Yes; no

b.) If so, did they think it was useful?

Yes; no; did not say

6. Would you tell others that you learned this information from the *yyy* show?

Yes; no

Applying Knowledge Gained from the Show

Shows often deal with situations that real people face in life. The following are some sample questions about applying knowledge from the show.

1. If a person who watches the *yyy* show regularly had a friend who wanted to adopt an HIV-positive child, what advice could he give to the friend (based on the show)?

2. If the friend wanted to know how crooks can cheat on real-estate deals, what could you tell him?

3. If you were on a plane that went down on a deserted island, what would you do to help ensure you are rescued quickly?

4. How does the show *Lost* deal with cultural differences? For example, how about the role of Asian women or Middle Eastern men?

5. If you were the president, how would you handle a situation where terrorists asked you to assist them in killing a foreign leader or risk the deaths of thousands of Americans?

6. If you didn't want your cell phone to be tracked by anyone, what would you do?

7. Occasionally, Jack Bauer tortures subjects to get information. What do you think of this policy and should the United States use it?

8. Does *The Simpsons* show present a realistic picture of middle-class family life?

9. If your friend asked you about the need to protect Americans' Second Amendment rights, how would you respond?

Specific Questions about the yyy Show

Here are some specific questions to ask about a particular show:

1. In a recent show, *xxx* happened. Tell me what you remember about that. What else? Why do you think that you remember that?

2. Are there any episodes that we haven't discussed already that you remember especially well? What are they? What do you remember about them? Why do you think you remember that?

3. Knowing a few facts about you is important for putting your answers into the right context.
   a.) Age
      18–25; 26–40; 41–60; over 61
   b.) Education
      High-school; some college; bachelor; post-bachelor
   c.) Interest in political news: local, state, national, international
      A lot, some, not at all

4. a.) Where do you go for political news?
      Newspaper, television, radio, the Web
   b.) How often do you read or watch the news?
      Regularly; occasionally

5. What types of news grab your interest? Let the respondent talk freely. Then follow with specific questions.
      Crime, war, human-interest stories, etc.

Appendix B
Directions for Analyzing
Message Boards

This appendix contains instructions for evaluating message board posts.

1. Check message boards for political/public policy content.
   a. How much is there—absolute and relative?
   b. How long are interaction threads?
   c. What topics are covered?
   d. Is there a discussion of values?
   e. How prevalent are emotional issues?
   f. How prevalent are emotional terms in discussion? Examples are "I feel" and "It makes me [happy, sad, angry, scared] that such and such is happening."
   g. How prevalent is discussion about what should be done about problems such as uninsured patients, youth crimes, police corruption, and environmental pollution?
   h. Do people relate the shows to real-world events? If so, is this prevalent or is it rare?
   i. Do they apologize about making a linkage to a fictional event?
2. Provide specific examples in each of your answers.

Appendix C
Directions for Coders of LexisNexis References

The following are instructions for performing a message-board type of analysis (see Appendix B) of LexisNexis references to the shows.

1. Check whether stories about the shows are in the entertainment section or general news section.
2. Check prominence factors, such as length of stories, headline size, front page placement, and editorial page placement.

NOTES

Chapter Two

1. This section has been adapted from an article published in *The Hedgehog Review*, 10(2): 36–47 by Doris A. Graber, in 2008, titled "Politics and the Media." The copyright is held by the Institute for Advanced Studies in Culture.

Chapter Three

1. We realize, of course, that the subjects' choices from their stored memories do not represent a full accounting.

Chapter Four

1. *Family Guy* turned out to be the least germane to our study, because the episodes running at the time said practically nothing about the current political scene.

2. The Middletown studies by Robert Staughton Lynd and Helen Merrell Lynd were sociological case studies of life in small-town America. The model for the prototype was Muncie, Indiana. The findings were published in two books: *Middletown: A Study in Modern American Culture* (1929) and *Middletown in Transition: A Study in Cultural Conflicts* (1937).

Chapter Five

1. The Netherlands has a population of 16.5 million citizens living in a densely populated total area of 34,000 square kilometers (21,127 square miles). Greece has 11.5 million people and a total area of 132,000 square kilometers (82,021 square miles).

2. Snowball sampling is a special nonprobability method that relies on referrals from initial subjects to generate additional subjects. It is often used in studies that aim to produce specific measures to be tested in larger samples (Salganik and Heckathorn, 2004).

3. All answers represent translations from the original local language texts.

4. The Eurobarometer survey was established in 1973 by the Public Opinion Analysis sector of the European Commission. It is an analysis of public opinion in all European Member States, and it addresses topics concerning European citizenship. For more information, see http://ec.europa.eu/public_opinion/index_en.htm.

REFERENCES

"An Inspired Presidential Choice." *Chicago Tribune*. 4-11-2006.

Alexander, Patricia and Philip Winne (eds.). 2006. *Handbook of Educational Psychology,* 2nd ed. Mahwah, N.J.: Erlbaum.

Anonymous. 1988. "The President's Night in the Sun." *New York Times,* 8-14-1988 editorial.

Barabas, Jason and Jennifer Jerit. 2010. "Are Survey Experiments Externally Valid?" *American Political Science Review,* 104(2): 226–242.

Bauerlein, Mark. 2008. *The Dumbest Generation: How the Digital Age Stupefies Young Americans and Jeopardizes Our Future.* New York: Penguin.

Baum, Matthew A. 2003. "Soft News and Political Knowledge: Evidence of Absence or Absence of Evidence?" *Political Communication,* 20(April/June): 173–190.
———. 2005. "Talking the Vote: Why Presidential Candidates Hit the Talk Show Circuit." *American Journal of Political Science,* 49(2): 213–234.

Baum, Matthew A. 2005. *Soft News Goes to War: Public Opinion and American Foreign Policy in the New Media Age.* Princeton, N.J.: Princeton University Press.

Baumgartner, Jody C. and Jonathan S. Morris. 2008. *Laughing Matters.* New York, Routledge.

Beavers, Staci L. 2002. "'The West Wing' as a Pedagogical Tool." *PS: Political Science & Politics,* 35(2): 213–216.

Bennett, W. Lance, Regina G. Lawrence, and Steven Livingston. 2007. *When the Press Fails: Political Power and the News Media from Iraq to Katrina.* Chicago: University of Chicago Press.

Bhatnagar, Namita, Lerzan Aksoy, and Selin A. Malkoc. 2004. "Embedding Brands Within Media Content: The Impact of Message, Media, and Consumer Characteristics on Placement Efficacy." In *The Psychology of Entertainment Media.* L.J. Shrum (ed.). Mahwah, NJ: Erlbaum: 99–116.

Blythe, Teresa. 2002. "Working Hard for the Money: A Faith-Based Media Literacy Analysis of the Top Television Dramas of 2000–2001." *Journal of Media and Religion,* 1(3): 139–151.

Bradley, Margaret, Maurizio Codispoti, Bruce N. Cuthbert, and Peter J. Lang. 2001. "Emotion and Motivation I: Defensive and Appetitive Reactions in Picture Processing." *Emotion*, 1: 276–298.

Bradley, Samuel D. 2004. "Decoupling Pacing and Information: An Embodied, Dynamic Account of Visual Perception and Memory." International Communication Association Convention paper.

Brants, Kees. 2004. "The Netherlands." In *The Media in Europe: The Euromedia Handbook*. Mary Kelly, Gianpietro Mazzoleni and Denis McQuail (eds.). Sage: London: 145–156.

Brown, Steven R. 2008. "Q methodology." In *The SAGE Encyclopedia of Qualitative Research Methods*. Lisa M. Given (ed.). Thousand Oaks, CA: Sage.

Cantor, Paul. 1999. "The Simpsons: Atomistic Politics and the Nuclear Family." *Political Theory*, 27(6):734–749.

Case, Donald O. 2007. *Looking for Information: A Survey of Research on Information Seeking, Needs, and Behavior, 2nd ed*. Amsterdam: Elsevier.

Chong, Dennis and James N. Druckman. 2010. "Dynamic Public Opinion: Communication Effects over Time." *American Political Science Review* 104(4): 663–680.

Christensen, Terry and Peter Haas. 2005. *Projecting Politics: Political Messages in American Films*. Armonk, NY: M.E. Sharpe.

Damasio, Antonio. 2003. *Looking for Spinoza: Joy, Sorrow, and the Feeling Brain*. Orlando: Harcourt.

Damasio, Antonio R. 1994. *Descartes' Error: Emotion, Reason, and the Human Brain*. New York: Grosset/Putnam.

———. 1999. *The Feeling of What Happens: Body Emotion in the Making of Consciousness*. New York: Harcourt.

Delli Carpini, Michael X and Scott Keeter. 1996. *What Americans Know About Politics and Why It Matters*. New Haven, CT: Yale University Press.

Delli Carpini, Michael X. and Bruce A. Williams. 2001. "Let Us Infotain You: Politics in the New Media Environment." In *Mediated Politics: Communication in the Future of Democracy*. W. Lance Bennett and Robert M. Entman (eds.). Cambridge, UK: Cambridge University Press: 160–181.

Demertzis, Nicolas. 1994. *The Greek Political Culture Today*. Papazissis Publishers: Athens.

———. 1997. "Greece." In *European Political Cultures: Conflict of Convergence*. Roger Eatwell (ed.). London: Routledge.

Edelman, Murray. 1985. *The Symbolic Uses of Politics*. Urbana: University of Illinois Press.

Entman. Robert M. 2005. "The Nature and Sources of News." In *Institutions of American Democracy: The Press*. Geneva Overholser and Kathleen Hall Jamieson (eds.). Oxford: Oxford University Press.

ER chat room. *The Strange Bedfellow,* episode 18. http://ertv.warnerbros.com.

Europa report, Eurobarometer 315.http://ec.europa.eu/public_opinion/archives/ebs/ebs_315_en.pdf.

European Commission, Public Opinion Archives: Eurobarometer 44.2, 2001. http://issda.ucd.ie/documentation/eb/s2828cdb.pdf.

Fields, Ingrid Walker. 2004. "Family Values and Feudal Codes: The Social Politics of America's Twenty-First Century Gangster." *The Journal of Popular Culture,* 37(4): 611–633.

Fitzgerald, Tony. 2005. "NBC Hurts But It's Still Got the Bucks." Media Life, April 19, 2005. http://www.medialifemagazine.com.

FootnoteTV. 2006. http://newsaic.com.

"Forensic science: The 'CSI effect.'" *The Economist,* April 22, 2010.

Franklin, Daniel P. 2006. *Politics and Film: The Political Culture of Film in the United States.* Lanham, MD: Rowman & Littlefield.

Gans-Boriskin, Rachel and Russ Tisinger. 2005. "The Bushlet Administration: Terrorism and War on The West Wing." *The Journal of American Culture,* 28(1): 100–113.

Gardner, Howard. 1975. *The Shattered Mind: The Person After Brain Damage.* New York: Vintage Books.

Gazzaniga, Michael S. 1992. *Nature's Mind: The Biological Roots of Thinking, Emotions, Sexuality, Language and Intelligence.* Harmondsworth: Penguin.
———. 1998. *The Mind's Past.* Berkeley, CA: University of California Press.

Gendler, Tamar Szabó and Karson Kovakovich. 2005. "Genuine Rational Fictional Emotions." In *Contemporary Debates in Aesthetics and the Philosophy of Art.* Matthew Kieran (ed.). Malden, MA: Blackwell.

Gilardi, Fabrizio. 2010. "Who Learns from What in Policy Diffusion Processes?" *American Journal of Political Science,* 54(3): 650–666.

Gilens, Martin. 2001. "Political Ignorance and Collective Policy Preferences." *American Political Science Review,* 95(2): 379–396.

Golding, William. 1954. *Lord of the Flies.* New York: Berkeley Publishing Group.

Goleman, Daniel. 1995. *Emotional Intelligence.* New York: Bantam Books.
———. 2006. *Social Intelligence: The New Science of Human Relationships.* New York: Bantam Books.

Gottlieb, Carl and Atiba Pertilla. 2001. "Quality Sells." Supplement to the November/December 2001 issue of *Columbia Journalism Review.*

Graber, Doris A. 2001. *Processing Politics: Learning from Television in the Internet Age.* Chicago: University of Chicago Press.
———. 2007. "The Road to Public Surveillance: Breeching Attention Thresholds." In *The Affect Effect: Dynamics of Emotion in Political Thinking and Behavior.* Ann Crigler, Michael MacKuen, George E. Marcus, and W. Russell Neuman (eds.). Chicago: University of Chicago Press: 265–290.
———. 2008. "Politics and the Media." *The Hedgehog Review,* 10(2): 36–47.
———. 2009. "Looking at the United States through Distorted Lenses: Entertainment Television Versus Public Diplomacy Themes." *American Behavioral Scientist,* 52(5): 735–754.

Green, Melanie C., Jeffrey J. Strange, and Timothy C. Brock (eds.). 2002. *Narrative Impact: Social and Cognitive Foundations.* Mahwah, NJ: Erlbaum.

Green, Melanie C., Jennifer Garst, and Timothy C. Brock. 2004. "The Power of Fiction: Determinants and Boundaries." In *The Psychology of Entertainment Media*. L.J. Shrum (ed.). Mahwah, NJ: Erlbaum: 161–176.

Holbert, R. Lance, Owen Pillion, David A. Tschida, Greg G. Armfield, Kelly Kinder, Kristin L. Cherry, and Amy R. Daulton. 2003. "The West Wing as Endorsement of the U.S. Presidency: Expanding the Bounds of Priming in Political Communication." *Journal of Communication*, 53 (3): 427–443.

Huckfeldt, Robert. 1979. "Political Participation and the Neighborhood Social Context." *American Journal of Political Science*, 23(3): 579–592.

Ignatieff, Michael, 1984. *The Needs of Strangers*. London: Chatto and Windus.

Ivanovich, David. 2005. "Senators seek answers to high natural gas costs; Road to new energy bill paved with responses" *The Houston Chronicle,* January 08, 2005.

Jamieson, Kathleen H. 2000. *Everything That You Think You Know About Politics ... and Why You Are Wrong*. New York: Basic Books.

Johnson, Steve. 2004. "Why 'Friends' Mattered ... but 'Frasier' was Better." *Chicago Tribune,* May 2, 2004.

Jones, Alex S. 2009. *Losing the News*. New York: Oxford University Press.

Jones, Gerard. 1992. *Honey, I'm Home!: Sitcoms, Selling the American Dream*. New York: Grove Weidenfeld.

Jones, Jeffrey P. 2005. *Entertaining Politics: New Political Television and Civic Culture*. Boulder, CO: Rowman & Littlefield.

Kalson, Sally. 2005. "Fictional Debate Easily Trumps the Real Thing." *Pittsburgh Post-Gazette*. 11-9-2005.

Kennedy, May G., Ann O'Leary, Vicki Beck, Katrina Pollard, and Penny Simpson. 2004. "Increases in Calls to the CDC National STD and AIDS Hotline Following AIDS-Related Episodes in a Soap Opera." *Journal of Communication,* 54: 287–301.

Keysers, Christian. 2010. "Mirror Neurons." *Current Biology,* 19 (21): R971–973. http://www.bcn-nic.nl/txt/people/publications/2009_Keysers_Current Biology.pdf.

Kozlowski, Dan. 2005. "Fans, Web Sites, and The West Wing: A Television Show Empowers and Inspires Its Constituency." Paper presented at the meeting of the International Communication Association in New York, May 2005.

Kull, Steven, Clay Ramsay, and Evan Lewis. 2003. "Misperceptions, the Media, and the Iraq War." *Political Science Quarterly,* 118(4): 569–598.

Lavery, David. 2002. "'Coming Heavy': The Significance of the Sopranos." In *This Thing of Ours: Investigating the Sopranos*. David Lavery (ed.). New York: Columbia University Press.

Lembo, Ron. 2000. *Thinking Through Television*. Cambridge, U.K. Cambridge University Press.

Liebes, Tamar and Elihu Katz. 1990. *The Export of Meaning: Cross-Cultural Readings of Dallas*. New York: Oxford University Press.

Loftus, Elizabeth F. 1996. *Eyewitness Testimony*. Cambridge, Mass: Harvard University Press.

Lombard, Matthew. 2010. Intercoder Reliability. http://www.temple.edu/sct/mmc/reliability/.

Lyrintzis Christos. 1984. "Political Parties in Post-Junta Greece: A Case of Bureaucratic Clientelism?" *West European Politics,* 7 (2): 99–118.

MacKuen, Michael, George E. Marcus, W. Russell Neuman, Luke Keele, and Jennifer Wolak. 2001. "Emotional Framing, Information Search, and the Operation of Affective Intelligence in Matters of Public Policy." MPSA Convention paper.

Mayer, Jane. 2007. "Whatever It Takes: The Politics Behind the Man." *The New Yorker,* February 19–26, 2007.

McClurg, Scott D. 2003. "Social Networks and Political Participation: The Role of Social Interaction in Explaining Political Participation." *Political Research Quarterly,* 56 (4): 449–464.

Milner, Henry. 1998. "Political Participation, and the Political Knowledge of Adults and Adolescents." Political Participation and Information workshop, 30th ECPR Joint Session of Workshops, University of Turin.

Mouzelis, Nicos. 1980. "Capitalism and the Development of the Greek State." In *The State in Western Europe.* Ray Scase (ed.). London: Croom Helm.

———. 1995. "Greece in the Twenty-First Century: Institutions and Political Culture." In *Greece Prepares for the Twenty-First Century.* Dimitris Constas and Theofanis Savrou (eds.). Baltimore and London: John Hopkins University Press.

Mouzelis Nicos and George Pagoulatos. 2002. "Civil Society and Citizenship in Postwar Greece." http://cde.usal.es/master_bibliografia/practicas/sistemas_comparados/grecia.pdf.

Murphy P. Karen and Lucia Mason. 2006. "Changing Knowledge and Changing Beliefs." In *Handbook of Educational Psychology,* 2nd ed. Patricia Alexander and Philip Winne (eds.). Mahwah, N.J.: Erlbaum.

Mutz, Diana C. 2001. "The Future of Political Communication Research." *Political Communication,* 18 (2): 231–36.

Mutz, Diana C. and Lilach Nir. 2010. "Not Necessarily the News: Does Fictional Television Influence Real-World Policy Preferences?" *Mass Communication and Society,* 13: 196–217.

Neuman, W. Russell. 1986. *The Paradox of Mass Politics: Knowledge and Opinion in the American Electorate.* Cambridge: Harvard University Press.

Neuman, W. Russell, George Marcus, Ann N. Crigler, and Michael MacKuen (eds.). 2007. *The Affect Effect: Dynamics of Emotion in Political Thinking and Behavior.* Chicago: University of Chicago Press.

North, Carol S. and Betty Pfefferbaum. 2002. "Research on the Mental Health Effects of Terrorism." *Journal of the American Medical Association,* 288: 633–636.

Page, Benjamin I. and Robert Y. Shapiro. 1992. *The Rational Public: Fifty Years of Trends in Americans' Policy Preferences.* Chicago: University of Chicago Press.

Papathanasopoulos, Stylianos. 2004. "Greece." In *The Media in Europe: The Euromedia Handbook*. Mary Kelly, Gianpietro Mazzoleni and Denis McQuail (eds.). London: Sage: 91–102.

Patterson, Thomas. 1993. *Out of Order*. New York: Knopf.

Pew Research Center for the People & the Press. 2001. "American Psyche Reeling from Terror Attacks." http://people-press.org/report/3/american-psyche-reeling-from-terror-attacks.

———. 2006. "Pew Research Center Biennial News Consumption Survey." http://www.pewinternet.org.

———. 2007. "Public Knowledge of Current Affairs Little Changed by News and Information Revolutions." http://www.people-press.org.

———. 2008a. "Financial Woes Now Overshadow All Other Concerns for Journalists." http://people-press.org/report/?pageid=1269.

———. 2008b. "Key News Audiences Now Blend Online and Traditional Sources: Audience Segments in a Changing News Environment." http://www.people-press .org/report/444/news-media.

———. 2008c. Biennial Media Consumption Survey 2008, Final Topline April 30–June 1, 2008. http://people-press.org/reports/questionnaires/444.pdf.

———. 2009. "Press Accuracy Rating Hits Two Decades Low." http://people-press.org/report/543/.

———. 2010a. "Political Knowledge Update." http://pewresearch.org/pubs/1668/political-news-iq-update-7-2010-twitter-tarp-roberts.

———. 2010b. "State of the News Media 2010." http://www.pewresearch.org/pubs/1523/state-of-the-news-media-2010.

Popkin Samuel L. and Michael A. Dimock. 1999. "Political Knowledge and Citizen Competence." In *Citizen Competence and Democratic Institutions*. Stephen L. Elkin and Karol Edward Soltan (eds.). University Park, PA: The Pennsylvania State University Press.

Potts, Kimberly. 2003. "Sopranos' Premiere Mobs Ratings." E! Online News, 9-17-2003. http://www.eonline.com.

Prior, Markus, 2004. "Visual Political Knowledge." http://www.princeton.edu/~mprior/Prior.Visual%20Knowledge.pdf.

Rosenstiel, Tom, Carl Gottlieb, and Lee Ann Brady. 2000. "Time of Peril for TV News: Quality Sells, But Commitment and Viewership Continue to Erode." *Columbia Journalism Review*, Special Report: Local TV News, 84–99, December.

Sachleben, Mark and Kevan M. Yeneral. 2004. *Seeing the Bigger Picture: Understanding Politics Through Film & Television*. New York: Peter Lang.

Salganik, Matthew and Douglas Heckathorn. 2004. "Sampling and Estimation in Hidden Populations Using Respondent-Driven Sampling," *Sociological Methodology*, 34: 193–239.

Salovey, Peter and John D. Mayer. 1990. "Emotional Intelligence." *Imagination, Cognition, and Personality*, 9: 185–211.

Scanlan, Stephen J. and Seth L. Feinberg. 2000. "The Cartoon Society: Using 'The Simpsons' to Teach and Learn Sociology." *Teaching Sociology*, 28(2): 127–139.

Schreiber, Darren. 2007. "Political Cognition as Social Cognition: Are We All Political Sophisticates?" In *The Affect Effect: Dynamics of Emotion in Political Thinking and Behavior.* W. Russell Neuman, George E. Marcus, Ann N. Crigler, and Michael MacKuen (eds.). Chicago: University of Chicago Press: 48–70.

Schudson, Michael. 1998. *The Good Citizen: A History of American Civic Life.* New York: Free Press.

———. 1999. "Good Citizens and Bad History: Today's Political Ideals in Historical Perspective." Unpublished paper. College of Mass Communication, Middle Tennessee University.

Shabecoff, Philip. 1988. "Congress Report Faults U.S. Drive on Waste Cleanup." *New York Times,* 6-18-1988.

Silverblatt, Art. 1995. *Media Literacy: Keys to Interpreting Media Messages.* Westport, CT: Praeger.

Skocpol, Theda and Morris Fiorina. 1999. *Civic Engagement in American Democracy.* Washington, D.C.: Brookings.

Sotiropoulos, Dimitris. 1995. "The Remains of Authoritarianism: Bureaucracy and Civil Society in Post-Authoritarian Greece." http://www.ceri-sciencespo.com/publica/cemoti/textes20/sotiropoulos.pdf.

Sotiropoulos, Dimitris A. and Evika Karamagioli. 2006. "Greek Civil Society: The Long Road to Maturity." Civicus Report. Access2democracy, Athens. http://www.civicus.org/new/media/CSI_Greece_Executive_Summary.pdf.

Specio, Michael L. and Ralph Adolphs. 2007. "Emotional Processing and Political Judgment: Toward Integrating Political Psychology and Decision Neuroscience." In *The Affect Effect: Dynamics of Emotion in Political Thinking and Behavior.* W. Russell Neuman, George E. Marcus, Ann N. Crigler, and Michael MacKuen (eds.). Chicago: University of Chicago Press: 71–95.

Stromberg, Peter G. 2009. *Caught in Play: How Entertainment Works on You.* Stanford, CA: Stanford University Press.

Swanson, David L., Ann N. Crigler, Michael Gurevitch, and W. Russell Neuman. 1998. "The United States." In *News of the World: World Cultures Look at Television News.* Klaus Bruhn Jensen (ed.). London: Routledge: 144–163.

Tenenboim-Weinblatt, Keren. 2009. "Where Is Jack Bauer When You Need Him? The Uses of Television Drama in Mediated Political Discourse." Political Communication, 26(4):367–387.

Thelen, David. 1996. *Becoming Citizens in the Age of Television.* Chicago: University of Chicago Press.

Thorndike, Edward L. 1920. "A Constant Error in Psychological Ratings." *Journal of Applied Social Psychology,* 4: 25–9.

Tsoukalas Constantine. 1981. "The Ideological Impact of the Civil War." In *Greece in the 1940s. A Nation in Crisis.* J.O. Iatrides (ed.). Hannover and London: University Press of New England.

Vig, Norman J. and Michael E. Kraft (eds.). 1990. *Environmental Policy in the 1990s.* Washington, D.C.: CQ Press.

Wallsten, Kevin. 2007. "How Conspiracies Rise, Spread and Fall: The Case of Voter Fraud, the Blogosphere and the 2004 Election." *Institute of Governmental Studies.* University of California, Berkeley, paper. http://repositories.cdlib .org/cgi/viewcontent.cgi?article=1145&context=igs.

Wattenberg, Martin. 2003. "Electoral Turnout: The New Generation Gap." *British Elections and Parties Review,* 13: 159–173.

Webster's Third New International Dictionary, Vol. II. 1966. Springfield, MA: G. & C. Merriam Co.

Yoshimine, Norikazu and Akifumi Tokosumi. 1999. "Toward A Cognitive Model of Empathy in Aesthetic Experience." http://www.jcss.gr.jp/iccs99OLP/ o3-02/o3-02.htm.

INDEX

About the Authors

Doris A. Graber is professor of political science and communication at the University of Illinois at Chicago. She has also taught at Northwestern University, the University of Chicago, and Harvard University's Kennedy School. She has written numerous influential articles and books on information processing, news media impact, and information policy issues, including *Mass Media and American Politics,* now in its eighth edition, and the prize-winning *Processing Politics: Learning from Television in the Internet Age.* She is founding editor of *Political Communication,* and book review editor of *Political Psychology.*

Tereza Capelos is Senior Lecturer of Political Psychology at Surrey University (United Kingdom). Previously, she held positions as assistant professor at Leiden University (Netherlands), and postdoctoral research associate at the Center for Survey Research at Stony Brook University (United States). Her research and publications focus on the affective and cognitive determinants of decision-making and policy evaluation.